MORE
GHOST STORIES
OF ALBERTA

MORE
GHOST STORIES
OF ALBERTA

BARBARA SMITH

LONE
PINE

THE PUBLISHER: **Lone Pine Publishing**

#206, 10426-81 Avenue	202A, 1110 Seymour Street	1901 Raymond Avenue SW, Suite C
Edmonton, Alberta	Vancouver, British Columbia	Renton, Washington
Canada	Canada	USA
T6E 1X5	V6B 3N3	98055

Canadian Cataloguing in Publication Data
Smith, Barbara, 1947-
    More ghost stories of Alberta

ISBN 1-55105-083-8
    1. Ghosts–Alberta. 2. Legends–Alberta. I. Title.
GR580.S641 1996   398.209712305   C96-910564-9

Senior Editor: Nancy Foulds
Editorial: Volker Bodegom
Design, Layout and Production: Gregory Brown
Printing: Webcom Ltd., Toronto, Ontario, Canada
Photos: Christina Dobson, p.138; Dobson Family photo, p.130;
Kent MacLeod, p.104; Robert Smith, p.15, 84, 99, 113, 117, 122, 127, 135,
141, 145, 153, 157, 172, 175, 193, 209; Deborah Trumbley, p. 194.

The publisher gratefully acknowledges the support of Alberta Community Development and the Department of Canadian Heritage.

DEDICATION

For my dear friend Denise Lyons and her three beautiful daughters, Sandra, Valerie and Joanne.

For my grandsons and for their peers – who will need forests as much as books – arrangements have been made to plant a sufficient number of trees to compensate for those used in printing this book.

CONTENTS

CHAPTER 4   THE SPIRIT'S INN

CHAPTER 5   EERILY ENTERTAINING

CHAPTER 6   SPIRIT SNIPPETS

CHAPTER 7   HOLY GHOSTS & SCHOOLS

ACKNOWLEDGEMENTS

Many people have contributed to this, my second collection of Alberta ghost stories. In compiling the book I've continued to count on friends and relatives who have kept the project in mind as they went about their daily routines. Their support has been deeply appreciated but it is the input from total strangers that has been most heartwarming to me. People have gone to an amazing amount of trouble in order to be of assistance. Often the assistance they were offering was so totally unselfish that they didn't even leave me their names. Some have stopped to chat as I visited book stores, others have called or written to radio and television stations after I've been interviewed and still others have contacted me through the publisher. To all of you anonymous contributors I say a warm and grateful "thank you."

Others have been equally helpful and have left me their names. I would like to take this opportunity to extend a public thank you to those folks: Diane Alexander of Edmonton, historian Tony Cashman, fellow author and ghost-story collector Jo-Anne Christensen, the ever-helpful Ron Hlady of Edmonton, Rob and Deb Isaac of Calgary, Elizabeth McLachlan of Provost, Don Morberg of Calgary, Marcella Robe, Bill Smith of Edmonton, Deborah Trumbley of Calgary and Deb Walker of Nanaimo, British Columbia.

There are two people who displayed almost overwhelming generosity: Jon Dolphin and Kathryn Carter, unbeknownst to each other and to me as well, were, at different times, also collecting local ghost stories. For very dissimilar reasons, both Jon and Kathryn abandoned their projects prior to publication. They did, however, keep their research material. Both these writers graciously donated ALL of their material to me. In a notoriously dog-eat-dog world, you two are extraordinarily kind people. I thank you both.

INTRODUCTION

Five years ago I worried that there wouldn't be enough Alberta ghost stories to fill a book. Today, I can only smile at my concerns. Almost as soon as my first book on ghosts in Alberta was published, I began receiving letters from people eager to tell me about their ghostly encounters. Many of those experiences had occurred years ago but the people had been hesitant to say anything to anyone for fear of being laughed at. Having read of others with similar tales to tell, they were now anxious to have someone listen to and record the unusual situations of which they'd been a part.

As a result, although I've met some fascinating folks, I'm certainly no wiser than when I began this quest. The stories I've been told and the additional research I've done have combined to pose more questions than they answered. Expected enlightenment often resulted in further mystification, leaving me with more unanswered questions about ghosts and hauntings than ever. I'm certainly no further ahead than I ever was in answering my questions "What is a ghost?" and "Why are they here?" or to solving the puzzle of why some people are more likely to see a ghost than others.

Over the years a number of interesting theories have been presented to address these questions. Frederic Myers, author of *Human Personality and Its Survival of Bodily Death* (1903) and one of the founding members of the old and honourable Society for Psychical Research in England, suggests that a ghost is "an indication that some kind of force is being exercised after death" and that this force "is in some way connected with a person" now deceased. He further purported that ghosts are unaware of themselves and incapable of thought.

Most other explanations are somewhat of a variation on the one presented by Frederic Myers. "Leftover energy" (physical or emotional) is a term used to describe the phenomenon that is a ghost. The "psychic imprint" theory holds that the essence of a person has been somehow stamped on the environment in which that person lived. The deceased person's soul has effectively left an imprint on the physical world.

Another theory holds that ghosts are disembodied souls (or energies, or personalities, or spirits) that are usually detectable only by our nearly redundant sixth sense. Rather than perceiving this otherworldly sensation with our familiar five senses, we notice the hair on our arms or the back of our necks standing up on end or tingling skin or the feeling that we are not alone or being watched.

Other students of the subject subscribe to the hypothesis that a ghost is a deceased person whose being either doesn't know he or she is dead or can't accept death because he or she feels obligated to complete unfinished business among the living.

Throughout all of these suppositions is the underlying question as to whether a ghost originates with the living person who is experiencing the encounter or with the ghost itself. Perhaps that point is debatable, but because many people report seeing or sensing the same spirit either at the same time or at different times, the event is certainly more objective than merely a figment of "the mind's eye."

The most strikingly different of all the theses is that of retrocognition—seeing or sensing the past. Chapter 7 of this book contains an excellent example of this phenomenon: during a family's visit to the Dunvegan Rectory historical site, two of the four members experienced retrocognition and were treated to a real glimpse of Alberta's past.

Another concept of a ghost is almost the opposite of retrocognition. Forerunners are sightings that lead people to predict future events. Undeniably some ghosts, such as forerunners, have messages for us, but others just seem to be continuing on about their business oblivious to the world of the living that surrounds them.

Despite this lack of agreement about what a ghost might be, their existence is attested to in all cultures and throughout history. My own experience collecting ghost stories has taught me one other consistency—that a paranormal encounter is a deeply moving experience. I have yet to have a story told to me in a flippant or even matter-of-fact way. Experiencing a ghost is clearly a profound occurrence in a person's life. Out of respect for this I have agreed to protect a contributor's anonymity when they have requested I do so.

Encountering a ghost is an event that some people are much more likely to experience than others. I have heard the suggestion that some of us are more tuned to the wavelength on which ghosts transmit. Although this attribute seems to be naturally occurring, it is also apparent that the ability can be either enhanced or diminished with practice.

Being haunted is not necessarily a permanent status for either person or place. For instance, Peter, the spirit that once added considerable spice to everyone's life around McKay Avenue School, Edmonton Public Schools' Museum and Archives, is now either keeping a very low profile or has moved on. Ron Hlady, an employee at the beautiful old school, reports that everything is "very quiet" these days.

Conversely other ghosts are incredibly tenacious. The ghosts of Roman soldiers are still occasionally spotted roaming the English countryside where they battled centuries ago. These reports, though, are old for contemporary times. As I have never heard or read of any place or person being haunted by the ghost of a caveman, I presume that, like all forms of energy, ghosts eventually weaken to the point of virtual dissipation.

If a place is haunted or if a ghost is present, predictable and distinguishable changes will usually be noted. These could include a dramatic temperature drop. This sudden coldness could be very localized or encompass a larger area. There may be drafts or odours or noises— all of which are apparently sourceless.

An issue of semantics arises in the re-telling of these stories. There are few true synonyms in the English language but I have chosen to use the following words interchangeably: spectre, spirit, entity, presence, phantom and ghost. (I was informed once that the term "ghost" is an inherently insulting one. I hope that this is not so, because I certainly mean no offence when I use the term.)

While apparitions and poltergeists also fall under the broad definition of the word ghost, they have some additional qualities. An apparition is a visible presence; it has a discernible physical form. Although this tends to be the popular conception of a ghost, an actual sighting (that is, an apparition) is actually a statistical rarity.

A poltergeist is an equally rare type of spectral being which can be identified by its noisy and possibly violent behaviours. It will often move objects and can actually wreak havoc on its surrounding physical environment. Poltergeists are strongly associated with people rather than places. They have been known to follow people for years even through a succession of moves.

❧

The ghost stories found in this book are not works of fiction. As a result they tend to be more ragged than we'd like them to be. A fictional account of a haunting will have a nicely structured and highly satisfying presentation—a beginning, a middle and an end. The anecdotes recorded here refuse to be that tidy—they are often merely fragments. This can be somewhat frustrating in a world so fond of neatness. We like to have any loose ends bound up by the last sentence—it's more satisfying that way. These, however, are reports of real events and we all know that life as we live it is anything but neat and tidy. I consider myself merely a recorder of events and so I have resisted the temptation to craft any of the stories in order to make them conform to an expected standard. A few readers have told me they find this frustrating. I can certainly sympathize although, by now, I tend to view the parts of the puzzle that are missing as being as provocative as those that have remained. You will notice my insertions of explanatory notes within quoted passages through my use of square brackets.

Of course I'm often asked if I've ever seen a ghost. The implication perhaps is, am I following that well-established rule of writing about what I know. The short answer is "no." I'm afraid that in the field of the paranormal I have few first-hand qualifications. It is merely my love of social history, in addition to a lifelong fascination with the possibility that ghosts might exist, that has brought me to write these books. For those who want a more exotic answer, or perhaps a more exotically qualified author, I offer the following anecdote.

The house where I live may, occasionally, have an invisible visitor. No one in our household smokes and yet we periodically smell cigarette smoke wafting through the place. The first few times this happened we would search the whole house thoroughly—not to find the smoking ghost but to make sure there wasn't a fire somewhere. Despite dozens of searches nothing ever turned up. Eventually we noted that this only began to happen after my earlier book on ghosts was released. There is a story in that book about our next door neighbour's house being haunted by the owner's late husband, a man named Bill. Once we became used to the experience, my husband and I decided, somewhat arbitrarily, that it was Bill's spirit that we occasionally detected. We were very happy with that conclusion—we no longer had to look for nonexistent fires in the house and we knew Bill's spirit was very protective of his widow and her house so we presumed he was a positive, if fleeting, addition to our household. We lived happily with that assumption for years, When we smelled the cigarette smoke we'd just smile at one another and calmly announce "Bill's here again."

That solution to the mysterious smoky smell worked well until I mentioned it to my neighbour, Bill's widow. Unfortunately, she knocked the comfort completely out of our theory with one short sentence—"Bill never smoked." There we were back at square one, having absolutely no idea why our house would, at times, smell strongly of cigarette smoke. Obviously I believe in the concept of ghosts and based on that I've made some optimistic guesses about our invisible smoker's identity but, for today, that's the closest I can come to a personal ghost story.

⚜

This collection is not an attempt to alter anyone's personal belief systems with my convictions or explanations. My intent is merely to entertain and possibly provoke thought in areas you might not explore. I do not pretend to be an educator but if reading this book introduces you to facets of Alberta's history and geography with which you were previously unfamiliar, then I am delighted.

I have purposely not included any tales of Native spirits, because I am not qualified to write them. Another category of ghost story that is missing from this book is one I was actively pursuing. I really wanted to find at least one story of phantom lights somewhere in Alberta—I didn't. Those ghostly lights are often associated with maritime stories but as they exist in Saskatchewan, which, of course, is just as land-locked as we are, that cannot be their sole cause. Despite this I have never heard an Alberta story that includes the phenomenon of apparently sourceless lights.

There were other disappointments in my research. For instance, try as I might I could not find anyone who knew the full story of the lady in white who is said to walk the Dunvegan Bridge, nor clarification of the rumour about a dark man in a Panama hat who haunts Bowness, or the burning house near the Leslieville side road by Rocky Mountain House, or the woman murdered by her husband who reportedly wanders the streets of Medicine Hat. Cobblestone Manor in Cardston is said to be haunted by Henry Hoet, its eccentric builder, and I have been told there is a house in Alix so haunted that when someone left a tape recorder running in the house the tape sounded as though the spirits were grabbing the microphone away from each other in order to have an additional turn recording their voice.

These all sound like marvelous stories but despite my best efforts, I'm disappointed to say that the book must go to print without them. If anyone knows about any of these stories, please feel free to contact me through Lone Pine Publishing. I'd love to hear from you. In the meantime do enjoy these Alberta ghost stories.

CHAPTER 1

HAUNTED HOUSES

THE GHOST OF THE PMQ

Imagine having to make room in your life for a ghost with a penchant for performing Uri Geller sorts of tricks. Don and Bobbie Miller lived with just such a spirit during their first year in Edmonton. In 1982, Don was a search-and-rescue technician recently transferred to Canadian Forces Base Edmonton. The strange incidents the couple experienced over those first few months at their PMQ (permanent married quarters) have left an indelible impression on their memories. They also remember their hesitancy to discuss the phenomenon with anyone.

"We kept the accounting pretty well to ourselves. The Armed Forces takes a dim view of their personnel seeing ghosts in the PMQs and then coming to work," the man explained before asking to be identified by a pseudonym. Given the intensity of the following story, his concerns about being identified were more than understandable.

In June of 1982, Don and Bobbie Miller were a young married couple with a four-month-old son. Don's career with the military meant frequent moves, and so when they were informed of the transfer to Edmonton, the couple accepted it as routine. And, for the first two months, it appeared that all was normal.

As they'd planned during her pregnancy, Bobbie stayed home to care for their son, Philip. This meant that the young mother was in the house a great deal, and because she hadn't had time to make new friends, she was often by herself with the baby. What might have been a lonely time for the woman was relieved by her thorough enjoyment of her new role as a mother and besides, for the first time in a long time, she was living close to relatives. Little did Bobbie suspect that she'd soon have even more in her life to ward off any possibility of loneliness.

The Millers are animal lovers and at that time they owned a very large cross-breed dog named Misty and a black cat named Willow. The animals were the first to realize that they were living in a haunted house. Despite numerous strange goings-on, the human members of the family weren't quite so easily convinced.

"At first it was always little things and we kept making excuses," Don said. "We had hung a dream catcher [a hoop ornamented with weaving, beads and feathers, of Native design, crafted to capture bad dreams] from the ceiling in one corner of the living-room," Don explained. "The dog and the cat would sit, absolutely motionless for hours, staring at that hoop."

At first merely puzzled by the animals' behaviour, Don and Bobbie were soon forced to accept that there was something abnormal occurring. The animals were definitely watching something that their owners could not see.

The dream catcher was a large one: its hoop measured about 30 centimetres across. It hung from the ceiling and twirled about freely whenever the furnace came on or a breeze blew through an open window. One day, however, Bobbie noticed the dream catcher turning when there were no drafts or air currents to propel it. Worse, although the device was turning in only one direction, the line on which it hung never shortened.

"Sometimes it would spin very fast, absolutely go crazy," Bobbie remembered. At the time she certainly never suspected that the ornament's activity was her introduction to life with an amazingly vigorous spirit. Despite its energy level, whoever or whatever the Millers shared their military-supplied home with apparently meant them no harm.

"There never seemed to be any malevolence or harm intended," they concurred. "These were more childish, attention-getting behaviours."

Bobbie's calm acceptance of its antics seemed to prompt the phantom into further tricks. Its next target was one with which many spectres enjoy tinkering—the television set.

"It was an old television. The channel selector was the old rotary type. It didn't turn easily," Don explained, adding that the dial was so stiff that it turned with more of a clunk than a click.

One evening, as Don sat enjoying a television show, the channel selector suddenly turned to another setting. Annoyed by the disruption to his viewing, Don switched the knob back to where it had been. Like his wife, he never suspected at the time that he'd just had his first experience with a ghost. He didn't report his experience to Bobbie for a few days and by then the channel-changing had become annoyingly frequent.

After a few sessions of unwanted channel surfing, accompanied by a spinning dream catcher, however, the two began to discuss the strange events they'd each noted but had never mentioned.

"It happens all the time," Bobbie responded when Don told her about his experience with the television dial.

"Bobbie was very comfortable with the whole thing," Don said. "I wasn't. I wasn't scared by it, I just wasn't very comfortable. The next time the dial on the television moved, I got mad."

This time, rather than get up and turn the selector back to the channel he'd been watching, Don exclaimed, "I own the television, now turn the damn thing back."

As he watched, the dial moved back to where it had been. From that point on, the paranormal activity in the nondescript PMQ duplex was continual. "There was always something," Bobbie added.

There were two bedrooms in the house, both on the second floor. "We used the room across from our bedroom as a combination spare room, storage, sewing and utility room," Don said. One reason that room was chosen as the spare room was it always felt cold. Neither of the Miller's pets would go into the room. It was one of the ghost's favourite places.

"We kept photo albums in the closet in that room. In one of the albums Bobbie kept the snapshots and postcards she'd brought back from her trip to Germany. A few of those pictures from the albums began turning up on the guest bed in that room," Don recalled.

No one else had been upstairs in their home and so Bobbie asked her husband if he'd gotten the pictures out. When he told her that he hadn't, she re-filed them into their allocated spots. She wrote the incident off as best she could while nevertheless acknowledging the growing collection of bizarre events she'd experienced in her new home.

The pictures being laid out on the bed soon became as regular as the dream catcher's unprovoked twirling. By the time the same two pictures had appeared on the bed several times, Bobbie was convinced that Don was playing a practical joke on her. She was annoyed and took the incident up with her husband.

"I knew I wasn't doing it, so I told Bobbie to wait until I was gone to work one day and then hide the photographs somewhere and don't tell me where they were. That way when they reappeared, she'd know for sure I had nothing to do with it," Don said. "Sure enough, two days later, there they were on the bed. It was always the same ones, too."

By then, the spare room had become a focal point for increased paranormal activity. The Millers owned a very old, heavy Underwood typewriter, which they kept in that room. It sat on top of an antique sewing-machine cabinet.

"One day I walked past the doorway to the spare room and there was the typewriter—on the floor," Bobbie remembered. There was certainly no way a machine weighing at least 13 or 14 kilograms could have fallen from its stand without Bobbie hearing it. Besides, it's doubtful that it would have landed in such a nice, neat, upright position right beside the sewing-machine. Not knowing what else to do, the woman lifted the old typewriter back onto the sewing-machine cabinet. At the time she could not have imagined all the ghostly goings-on that would soon revolve around that antique typewriter, nor that the resident spirit's strength was steadily increasing. There was much more to come for the Millers and their military housing.

The dream catcher still spun frequently for no apparent reason and the family pets still stared intently in that direction for hours. Willow, the cat, however, would also stare into the upstairs room, in much the way that she did in the one corner of the living-room. Misty's reaction was even more interesting. The well-trained and normally obedient dog absolutely refused to enter the spare room no matter how he was coaxed or ordered. Both animals clearly sensed something very strange in the room.

It seemed that just as Don and Bobbie became adjusted to each of the spirit's high jinks, it added another one to its repertoire. Despite the spirit's determination to attract attention to itself, it only allowed itself to be seen once, just for a few seconds, if in fact it even was the same spirit.

One morning, as he stood at the top of the stairs looking down, Don saw what he thinks might have been the poltergeist. "She was standing at the bottom of the stairs. She was slender and had shoulder-length hair. She wore a dark dress with flowers," he recalled. Utterly astonished by what he was seeing, he wanted to share the experience with Bobbie and yet, "I had the sense that if I turned away the ghost wouldn't be there when I turned back."

And that is exactly what happened. Although deeply disappointed that his wife wasn't able to see the image, Don's convictions never wavered. "I stand by what I saw," the no-nonsense man stated firmly.

Given the contradiction between the image Don saw and the type of ghostly activity they'd been experiencing, it's possible that the apparition at the bottom of the stairs was another, more passive spirit. She may have been in the house all along or she may just have been passing by that one morning.

Bobbie may not have seen the image that Don did, but she continued to be very aware of a presence in her home. She took to glancing into the spare room each time she passed it and when she found the typewriter on the floor, she would calmly put it back onto the sewing-machine cabinet. Then, while going about her chores on the main floor of the house one day, Bobbie heard the readily identifiable sound of typing coming from upstairs. That was enough. Thinking that taking it out of the spare room would end the activity with the typewriter, she lugged the heavy old machine down to the basement and set it in the floor. At least here it couldn't fall again. The relocation, however, didn't stop the sounds of typing.

During this period the quality of the Millers' life began to slip. "It was a stressful time," Bobbie confirmed.

As a search-and-rescue technician, Don was obligated to stay in excellent physical condition, and previously he'd taken pride in his good health. Soon, despite paying the same amount of attention to his well-being that he always had, Don's health started to suffer. He began to experience a string of unrelated illnesses and at one point was even hospitalized. At the time the couple didn't associate Don's declining health with their undeniably strange living conditions. In retrospect, however, they are suspicious that the two were connected.

For the time, however, the Millers could do little but struggle on as best they were able. The photographs continued to appear on the bed in the spare room and the dream catcher continued its unprovoked spinning. The typewriter, even from its new station in the basement, continued to sound as though someone was typing on it when no one (visible) was anywhere near the machine.

One day, while listening to the typewriter keys clunking away rhythmically downstairs, Bobbie got an idea. Later that day, when all was quiet, she went into the basement and rolled a fresh piece of paper into the typewriter. Oddly, it seemed that inserting the paper apparently stopped the spirit's interest in the typewriter—at first anyway.

For a while the Millers saw no new paranormal activity in their haunted house. Then, one morning when Bobbie came downstairs to make breakfast, she was greeted by a sight she can never forget. All the cutlery in the drawer was bent in half. Every knife, fork and spoon had effectively been folded over on itself. Presuming this mayhem to be the work of their resident phantom, Bobbie ordered the presence to repair the damage it had done. Then she went back upstairs and stayed there for some time, attending to more routine matters. When she returned to the kitchen, the cutlery had been straightened.

The ghost was clearly gaining power and once the Millers suspected that it had even followed them to the grocery store. As they pushed a shopping cart down an aisle, both Bobbie and Don felt a shove at the middle of their backs. They spun around, first to face each other, wondering whether the other one had also felt the force or even, perhaps, instigated it.

Who could possibly have pushed them? "There was no one there and we were in the middle of the aisle so there was no way anyone could have pushed us and then ducked around a corner," Don explained.

By now the two thought they were resigned to the spirit's high jinks. Then one day Bobbie's mother called. Knowing that Don would be working, she invited her daughter and grandson to come for dinner. Pleased to have the visit to look forward to, Bobbie returned to her day's routine. Not long afterwards she heard a noise coming from the basement. Someone or something was busy typing.

Revealing her admirably calm and accepting nature, Bobbie waited until the sounds stopped and then went down to the basement. Even from a distance she could see that there was a message on the piece of paper that she'd rolled into the machine weeks before. Her foresight had finally paid off. She pulled the sheet out from the roller and was immediately disappointed to discover she was not dealing with a deeply philosophical ghost. There, where all the answers to this world's great unknowns could have been revealed, was this simple message: *"HAVE A PLEASANT TIME AT YOUR PARENTS' HOME."*

Bobbie had just received a direct communication from the ghost she'd known for months existed. Admittedly a bit unnerved, the young woman's overriding feeling was one of frustration at the mundane nature of the message. It seemed nothing more than the ghostly equivalent of the standard, and virtually meaningless, "Have a nice day."

Although Bobbie never left paper in the typewriter again, she and Don both continued to hear the keys being depressed as the machine sat, unattended, on the floor in their basement. And they weren't the only ones to be aware of the PMQ's phantom typist.

Don explained, "In the summer of 1982 friends of ours moved from Cold Lake to Edmonton. Their son, Damion, would occasionally babysit our son. One evening while sitting, he became frightened. He heard the typewriter in the basement and went to check it out."

The young man stood and watched in horrified amazement as the typewriter's keys repeatedly depressed, one after another, as if an invisible typist was at work. Working conditions this spooky were more than

Damion could accept. He picked up Philip and bolted for the door. Fortunately, the safety of his own, unhaunted, home was nearby.

Throughout all these events, and because at the time she didn't connect Don's continuing health problems with the ghostly presence, Bobbie had remained unconcerned and went about life as though nothing out of the ordinary were happening.

"In a strange way it was company for me," she recalled. The persistent spirit in the PMQ, however, was about to go too far and lose Bobbie's acceptance.

"One afternoon I put the baby down for his nap. He was about six months old at the time. A couple of hours later I heard him waking up and went upstairs to get him out of his crib. Bobbie only got as far as the bedroom doorway—there, stacked neatly on top of Philip's bureau stood every article of clothing the baby owned. When the young mother had put her son into his crib earlier in the afternoon his clothing had been in the bureau drawers where it belonged. Even though all proud parents think their children are very advanced intellectually and physically, Bobbie knew that there was no way that six-month-old Philip would have been capable of even getting out of his crib, let alone opening dresser drawers and sorting through his own clothes until they stood in a pile.

The ghost had exceeded what her maternal instincts would allow by indicating an interest in her child. Bobbie Miller was ready to look for a new house. Don, who had never been as easygoing as Bobbie about living in a haunted house, concurred and, using the ruse of needing a roomier place, they began to inquire about some vacant houses on the base. Within a short time, they moved to the new place. Don's health began to improve noticeably, as did the family's overall contentment with life, as the couple put the past as far behind them as they could.

The couple who rented the Miller's former home, however, did not fare so well. Their marriage ended within six months of moving into the haunted residence. As it's not known whether the marriage was already in jeopardy when they moved into place, it's impossible to assess whether or not this PMQ's long-standing, usually invisible resident was a factor in the separation.

The dwelling is still standing and apparently occupied, but the Millers, who are no longer associated with the military and no longer live in Edmonton, haven't bothered checking into the supernatural activity level in their old home. It is clear, however, that the ghost did not follow them, for the Millers have gone on to lead happy, successful lives.

MISSING LINKS

On April 20, 1962, housewife Paris Willey phoned the Edmonton police to report her husband, Frank Willey, missing. To date, the man has not been located. All that ever turned up were pools of blood and minute particles of hair and fabric. That grisly evidence was discovered inside a partially constructed house in southeast Edmonton. It certainly wasn't much for the police to go on, but those findings were sufficient for them to conclude that Frank Willey had been murdered just hours before his wife telephoned them.

The case was a gruesome and convoluted puzzle. Frank had been a dashing figure, a well-liked professional golfer who routinely carried large sums of money. On the surface, Frank Willey appeared to have had it all. He was married, the father of two boys, happily employed and he owned a nicer-than-average home overlooking Edmonton's North Saskatchewan River. Now he had vanished.

In spite of extensive searches, Frank's body was never found. Amazingly, the police were still able to solve the crime. An intelligent and tenacious criminal investigation led to the arrests and eventual conviction of the murderers. The quiet capital of Alberta had never witnessed such a case before. Flamboyant characters, a love triangle, huge sums of money and a missing body all combined to create a ghoulishly interesting diversion for the general public.

Despite the clearly incriminating case the police built against them, neither Bill Huculak nor Ray Workman ever confessed to the murder of Frank Willey. Maintaining their innocence to the bitter end, they were each sentenced to a lengthy incarceration. Ray Workman, suspected leader of the two, died while serving his time, effectively making his term a life sentence.

One piece of the puzzle, however, remains missing to this day. Where is Frank Willey's body?

The Shaws of southeast Edmonton think they may know the answer. Mr Shaw, who prefers that his first name not be used, is a plumber. In the spring of 1962, while the intriguing case of the Frank Willey case swirled throughout the normally quiet government town, Mr Shaw was contracted to install the plumbing in a new house in the Fulton Place neighbourhood. When the general contractor who hired him went broke, Mr Shaw decided to buy the place. It would make an excellent home for his family, he reasoned and, because his employer needed money quickly, he could get it at a good price.

Mr Shaw, his wife, Edna, and their two children moved in shortly afterwards. From the day of the move it became apparent that they'd bought a haunted house. Between the arrivals of truckloads of furniture at their new house, Edna drove to a nearby restaurant to buy a meal of take-out food. She left her daughter to start unpacking. Edna returned some twenty minutes later to find a badly shaken daughter. The child had distinctly heard a tune being whistled. The music came from the basement. A thorough search turned up no possible source for the sounds.

From that first instance onwards, something or someone seemed to be trying to demonstrate its presence. When the children's grandparents stayed in the home to babysit, they frequently heard the very distinctive sound of the garage door being opened. At each occurrence they checked the attached garage and found the door closed, as it had been left.

The family occasionally heard footsteps coming up the basement stairs. Once, after watching the doorknob turning, Edna Shaw ran to it and swung the door open. There was no one there—no one that she could see.

Children in the neighbourhood reported to the Shaws that via an Ouija board they'd contacted the ghost that haunted their house and that he'd identified himself by the initials F.W. Following that incident, the couple tried to get their resident spirit to make himself known more clearly to them. His only reply to their invitation seemed to be a continuation of his high jinks.

Mr Shaw operated his plumbing business from the house. He kept petty cash for the company in a strongbox. It was always locked and only Edna knew the combination. When the woman returned from a trip and opened the box, she found all the coins in it neatly sorted and stacked. She had not left them that way.

"We always felt he went out of his way to make his presence known to us," the woman explained. "But he never made us feel uncomfortable."

Perhaps this lack of discomfort is more a credit to the Shaw's ability to take life's oddities in stride than to any intention on the ghost's part. Few people could have related the following incident as calmly as the Shaws did: In a rarely used section of the basement, Edna found a cotton comforter that the family had been storing. It had been unrolled and was now lying on the cement floor. There was an imprint of a body in the centre of the material. Not wanting an untidy home, Edna Shaw bent to re-roll the blanket. Where the imprint of the body was, the comforter had adhered to the floor.

The community of Fulton Place is situated a short distance from the house where Frank Willey was murdered. At the time of his murder, the Shaw's future home was nearing completion. The ground that would soon become the garage pad had been loosened, levelled and roped off in preparation for the concrete truck's arrival. It would not have required much effort for Workman and Huculak to dig a shallow grave in the prepared soil, deposit the golfer's body into the hollow and replace the dirt. Subsequently, the unsuspecting concrete-pouring crew would, effectively and permanently, hide the evidence of Workman's and Huculak's murderous deed.

When the Shaw family decided to sell the haunted house, the decision had nothing to do with its resident spirit. It was merely time to move on. Today the house remains occupied and on a recent drive past the address, renovations were noted. The garage, under which Frank Willey's body likely lies entombed, is now a cozy-looking family room.

It's not known whether or not the spirit of the murdered man performs his attention-getting high jinks for the new owners...or whether he's gone on to play golf into eternity.

NEGATIVE, NOISY SPIRIT

While collecting ghost stories over the years, I have been interested to occasionally note the emergence of patterns. For instance, a sudden drop in temperature is a strong indication of the presence of a spirit. Another common theme is the sensitivity of children to paranormal activity. I have also heard a number of stories that indicate that the intensity of a haunting can increase or decrease depending on the atmosphere created in the home—sufficient amounts of positive energy can apparently overpower a negative presence in a home.

A young woman once confided that she suspected that there had been a malevolent spirit in the house that she and her husband had purchased a few years before. The couple had always enjoyed a positive relationship until they moved into their new house. After the move, the bond soured almost immediately and the two began fighting.

"We actually split up at one point," she told me. "Fortunately, we were able to work things out. We still live in the house and we're happy there now but it really did feel as though we overcame some kind of a negative force in that house. It was just so uncomfortable in there at first. We knew when we bought it that the reason the house was for sale was because the couple who had owned it had separated. I always wondered about that."

In another example of this phenomenon, a story in this book ("The House Had an Evil Spirit," p. 32) tells of a youngster being aware that there was something malignant in a small section of his family's home. After being occupied by a large, boisterous family for many years, the house sat vacant for at time. When the young man returned, intending only to sleep overnight at the old family homestead, he found that the negative presence that had once been confined to a small area had grown in both intensity and size to such a degree that he could not stay there.

I suspect the following haunted house story reflects much the same phenomenon.

Darwin Christensen began his explanation of the events that he had endured with a disclaimer of sorts. He told me, "I had lived in that house for nine years. These definitely weren't 'house noises' I was hearing. I knew the noises that house made."

The house in question is about forty years old, a bungalow divided into two suites. Darwin was only seventeen and just out of high school when he and a friend moved into the basement suite.

"By the second summer, my friend had moved out, so I was alone there. I was working as a landscaper and at the time I was really into jogging and reading and enjoying being by myself. One afternoon I was lying on my bed reading and I drifted off to sleep," he related.

Darwin's nap was short-lived, however. "I woke up to see the figure of a woman at my bedroom door." More embarrassed than frightened, he pretended to still be asleep. "I rolled over before I looked again. She was gone," Darwin explained, before repeating for emphasis, "There was a figure there."

Not long after that brief encounter, Darwin's sister, Jo-Anne, moved to Edmonton and the two took over the upstairs apartment in the house. Both brother and sister are equally friendly and outgoing and so for years the little house was a busy place, the venue for many happy times.

Eventually Jo-Anne met her future husband, Dennis. As the basement apartment was vacant once again, Darwin moved back downstairs and left the upstairs for the newlyweds. The slightly extended family continued to live and entertain happily under one roof until Jo-Anne and Dennis were expecting their first child. They decided that the rented accommodation they'd enjoyed calling home for so long was no longer suitable. They bought a place of their own and moved out, leaving Darwin almost back where he started, alone in the basement apartment. Darwin knew, however, that he too would soon be moving. He and his girlfriend were planning a trip to Europe after which they hoped to find an apartment together.

"I was rarely home during that time," Darwin recalled. "I was working so much. I didn't even eat there. The place began to feel gross. Just ugly. It felt moist and dark and chilled. Jo-Anne and I had been there for years but now the house was just empty, void of life. It was always cold in that place."

To make matters worse, Darwin's girlfriend was living and working in Vancouver at the time. As many couples in long-distance relationships do, the two began to experience problems. It was then that Darwin started to hear strange sounds from the empty upstairs suite.

"Before they left, Jo-Anne and Dennis had taken the shower doors off the bathtub and had left them leaning against a wall. It sounded as though those doors had fallen. I thought I heard them falling, scraping against the wall and then landing on the floor with a bang but the noise wasn't quite loud enough."

After listening to exactly the same noise three or four times in a week Darwin decided he should investigate.

"I still had a key to the upstairs so I went up. The shower doors were still there leaning up against the wall. They hadn't slid down and there was nothing else in the house [that might explain the noise]."

Puzzled and increasingly uncomfortable, Darwin returned to his own apartment.

A few days later, Darwin's girlfriend called from Vancouver. The conversation didn't go well and soon a serious argument developed. The presence that had been causing the unnerving scraping and banging sounds apparently responded to all this negativity with increasing strength.

"This time [the noise] was so loud that I wondered if a tree had hit the house. It was the same sound only much louder."

The scraping was still there but this time, rather than being followed by a bang, it was followed by a loud boom.

"I began to realize the noises were coinciding with me feeling bad. It really scared me," Darwin recalled. "We hung up then but she called back and we continued the argument. As we talked there were more scrapes and booms. The sound was coming from right over top of my head. I thought, 'Wow, this is scary.' And I knew it wasn't my imagination because my cat was responding to the sounds too and at one point the cupboard doors in my bathroom vibrated from one of the booms."

Eventually both the long-distance argument and frightening sounds ended for the night. However, "The next day I was going over the phone call in my mind and the sounds started all over again," Darwin remarked.

Darwin had been trying to explain his experiences to his friends but the others put little stock in his reports—until he invited three of them over for dinner a few nights later.

"I'd been telling them about the noises and before we ate I showed them the empty apartment upstairs. About halfway through the meal it started. Scrape. Boom." Darwin raised his voice for emphasis. "I'd described the sounds so well that [my friends] recognized them."

Once the presence had the young men's attention, it apparently wasn't going to let up. "It did it again during coffee but not so loud that time," Darwin affirmed.

After sharing the frightening experience with Darwin, his friends were no longer so anxious to disregard his anecdotes.

Not surprisingly, Darwin made an effort to spend as little time as possible at home. After three and a half months of torment by an unseen but very noisy and responsive presence, he said goodbye to the place. As planned, Darwin and his girlfriend boarded a plane for Europe. Upon their return, the two found an apartment together.

Their new place isn't too far from the little bungalow that had been Darwin's home for so many years. He still drives past the old place occasionally and was interested to note that there were new tenants, but only for a couple of weeks. Whoever moved in after him apparently moved back out again very quickly. Since then the place has been sitting empty...maybe.

NO LASTING EFFECTS

Folklore buff Kathryn Carter added this story to the collection. She spoke with the young woman who'd had the experience related below. At the time Anna asked to be identified only by her first name.

When seven-year-old Anna and her family moved to a house in Edmonton's west end, neither the child nor her parents had any way of knowing that the move would bring about an experience of dark terror. They had no idea that a small area in their new home was haunted.

Anna recalled that she had always felt frightened in the master bedroom of the house. Although she couldn't say why, the room filled her both with an inexplicable sense of dread and with a strange sense of fascination.

The family had lived in the house for only for a few months when little Anna wandered away from the breakfast table. None of the family paid any attention to the girl's departure. They didn't know that an unseen force was drawing the child to the closet in her parents' bedroom.

Anna opened the closet door. It was as dark inside as she'd expected it would be. Then, to the child's horror and amazement, the back of the closet became deeper and blacker until it became a dark swirling hole. The little girl stood paralyzed with fear as two hands reached out to her from the eddy of blackness. Grabbing at Anna's clothes, the hands tried to pull her into the ominous void.

The child's terrified screams brought her parents running to her rescue. Her mother reached her first. As the startled woman asked her daughter what was wrong, the girl felt the hands release her. The dark, swirling vacuum of darkness then sealed itself.

Naturally enough, Anna's mother tried to console her daughter with reassurances that the incident had been just a figment of her overactive, childish imagination, but Anna stuck to her story. The fear she felt anytime she went near that bedroom bore witness to the reality of the event. When nothing would assuage the child's terror, her parents began to investigate the history of the house. Police records eventually confirmed the stories that neighbours had relayed about the violent parties that had once gone on in the house. One drunken brawl had even ended in murder when a man had stabbed another to death—in the master bedroom.

Happily, Anna is now a vibrant and accomplished young woman. Clearly, she suffered no lasting effects from the experience with the evil entity in the closet.

THE HOUSE
HAD AN EVIL SPIRIT

Often spirits are associated only with one area of a building. A presence that is felt distinctly in one room will be totally absent in an adjoining one. Sometimes this phenomenon is puzzling but, in this story from Rocky Mountain House, there seems to be quite a reasonable explanation.

"It was an old house, which had been built, so I am told, by adding on bits and pieces of other buildings to the original, central room of the house," explained Gordon Jackson, who was raised in the partially haunted house. "The incidents that I am about to tell you about happened in the part of the house that used to be my brother's bedroom."

Gordon couldn't recall exactly how old he was when he first realized that there was something unnatural about his family's acreage home. He surmised, however, that he would have been roughly just preschool age.

"I remember quite vividly going into my brother's bedroom and going into the closet for something. When I opened the closet door, I remember seeing a face, a horrifying face, a definitely evil face."

All but paralyzed with fear, Gordon fled from the room. "I remember that I had thought it was my sister playing a terrible trick on me and that I had been even more terrified when I saw her sitting in the living-room with my mother."

The human psyche will try to repress what it's not capable of dealing with and to some extent Gordon's young mind was successful. "I have since forgotten what the face actually looked like, which is fine by me," he confirmed. "I have never forgotten the feeling of terror that it gave me and ever after that I was never comfortable in that section of the house," he added.

This feeling persisted for the youngster even though his parents had the house completely renovated and what was once his brother's bedroom became the pantry.

"The way the renovations had been done, you had to go through the kitchen and pantry to get to the bathroom and I remember many times running from the bathroom through the pantry in a panic, sure that something was after me, and then collecting myself in the kitchen so I could enter the living-room where my parents sat, so that I didn't look like a fool," Gordon admitted.

Gordon Jackson lived with this sense of an evil presence in one area of his family's home until he left the fold. By the mid-1980s, both of Gordon's parents had died and he was a college student living in Edmonton. During a break from school, he returned to Rocky Mountain House and the home he'd been raised in.

"Although I still owned the property, it was closed up and had not been lived in for several years," he explained. What happened next indicates that, in his enumeration of the occupants, the young man may have overlooked the home's tenant of longest standing—the ghost.

Like students everywhere, Gordon was very conscious of the need for thrift. "I decided that I would camp out in the house, thus saving money."

Unfortunately, his best intentions to serve the dual purposes of saving money and coming to grips with whatever had interfered so badly with his serenity during his formative years were not to turn out too well. "I didn't even last long enough for true night to fall, I was out of the house before twilight was over," he explained, looking back on the experience.

"I remember quite strongly the smell of damp and disuse that greeted me when I opened the door," he recalled. "and the frigid air that rushed past me. I very nearly left right then and in retrospect I wish I had."

Gordon Jackson persisted with his plan, however. "I set up camp in the living-room. This was the original central building and it had its own door, the front door. I cooked and ate supper outside, on the porch that was attached to the front door and everything was fine while I was outside. It was only when I returned to the living-room inside [that] things began to happen."

The next sensation that Gordon experienced was one that people who've had encounters with the paranormal almost always report. He explained it as "a sort of something's watching you feeling." Showing amazing courage and determination, Gordon turned to face in "the direction I perceived the uneasiness as coming from."

A mental duel of sorts began—courage against supernatural terror. "The uneasiness began to grow stronger and stronger," he recounted, "as if whatever was causing it was drawing nearer and nearer."

Gordon looked past the living-room into two adjoining rooms, both with windows facing the same direction. "The light from outside, though dim, was still bright enough for me to make out details in both rooms. Then I noticed the light in the kitchen was growing steadily darker and darker and the light in the [other]room was staying the same!"

Temporarily rooted by sheer terror, Gordon analyzed the situation. "Anything outside affecting the light should be affecting both [rooms] the same, or if something were blocking the light by standing in the kitchen window, it should have been visible."

With chilling descriptive powers, Gordon continued. "Instead it seemed as though the darkness was gathering between the window and the doorway, gathering where [as a child] I saw the face connected to the bathroom where I always felt a cold and prickly feeling, as if something was watching me."

Gordon endured the horror-filled sensation for as long as he could—for just seconds, he reported. "Then the darkness slowly made a move toward the living-room and my feet took over. I paused only long enough to lock the door behind me."

Clearly, whatever the presence was, it certainly didn't want Gordon there, but at least it was content to remain in the house. "The overwhelming sense of fear eased considerably once I was out of the house," he explained.

Despite this relief, it took a while for Gordon to settle down. "It wasn't until I reached the end of the driveway and was on my way back into town that I really began to feel better. I went back the next day, with friends, in broad daylight to collect the gear that I had left there the night before, and even then I couldn't bring myself to go near the kitchen or the pantry. I just locked everything back up and left," Gordon affirmed. "I never looked back."

Gordon Jackson sold his rural real estate and tried to put the past entirely behind him. He remarked that "I have often wondered if whoever moved in after me has ever felt anything out of the ordinary, but I have never tried to find out."

To this day, Gordon has no idea whether or not he was the only one of his family to have terrifying experiences in the family home. Perhaps other family members also had encounters and, like he was, were hesitant to share the information. Perhaps in lieu of communication with others, the man has devoted considerable mental energy to rationalizing the events that took place in his childhood home.

"I have thought long and hard about [my strange experiences] and cannot come up with a solution that I can accept. In my heart I know that what I felt and saw was some evil presence that haunted...part of the house. I think that after the house was left empty, the presence grew stronger and more possessive and that it was not happy about the fact I intended to stay there," he concluded.

This is not the first time I've heard of hauntings, especially unpleasant ones, that have apparently gained in strength over the time that a house was unoccupied – by live people, that is.

HOUSE WITH AN AGENDA

Sandi Jackson now lives in Calgary, but in 1979 she and her parents lived for a time in a section of Red Deer called the Pines.

"The house was spectacular," she remembered, before relating some very dramatic instances that also set the house apart.

"About six months [after we moved in] my mother kept hearing footsteps throughout the house when she was home alone. On another occasion, the washing machine began its spin cycle," Sandi explained "even though the machine was not being used at the time."

In another incident, Sandi and her mother were alone in the house, sitting in the living-room and enjoying watching a television show.

"We heard a crack and watched a 2 metre indoor plant bend completely in half, then within seconds go right back up to its original state. That was enough for me," she confirmed. "I was half scared to death. I knew then…that something was very wrong in that house."

Sandi's conviction was strong enough that her parents were forced to listen to her concerns about their new house and they listed the place for sale.

"The day the for-sale sign went up on the lawn, the presence in the house threw us for a loop," she began. And apparently "us" in this case includes more than just the human members of the young woman's family. "Our cats went crazy. They hissed and growled and went absolutely wild in unison. Well, that was enough for me. I couldn't take it anymore. I stayed with my friend's family for the three weeks it took to sell the house," Sandi admitted.

The family sold the house to a man they knew, and he has lived in the posh house in the Pines ever since. However, "as far as we know, he has had no weird happenings in the last sixteen years. Perhaps the house was simply particular as to who could live in it," Sandi concluded.

MILL WOODS POLTERGEIST

Canadian suburbs bear striking similarities in design, no matter what city you're in. Edmonton's Mill Woods falls well within the expected pattern. From the outside, most of the houses there fit the mold.

Skeptic Wayne Ritchie lived next door to a house that was very different on the inside, however. As an Air Canada employee, the man worked some very strange shifts. After a long shift in the dead of winter, it was not unusual for Wayne to pull into his driveway at 4 AM. Had he not been coming and going at those hours, he might never have noticed that there was something decidedly unusual about the house next door to his.

Initially Wayne might have wondered if his neighbours were fresh-air freaks. Even on Edmonton's chilliest nights, their house would have at least one window open wide enough so that the curtains billowed out. While this trait certainly puzzled the man, it didn't really affect his life, so he dismissed it as evidence of some unknown idiosyncrasy.

When summer came, however, and Wayne's dog was spending more time out in the yard, whatever was odd about the neighbouring property became a more personal issue. The normally quiet and well-behaved dog would sit in the backyard, barking endlessly, for no apparent reason.

Despite this noisy irritation, Wayne didn't meet his new neighbours until their house developed a bizarre plumbing problem. The couple came to his door one day asking if he'd had any trouble with sewage backup. He assured them that he hadn't. In an effort to be helpful, he added that he owned a fairly extensive set of tools and had some knowledge of plumbing systems. He told them he'd be glad to try to help.

The couple gratefully took Wayne up on his generous offer and the trio made their way from Wayne's back door to the neighbour's bathroom with its overflowing toilet. There, sometime later, they discovered the cause of the blockage—a large beefsteak had been stuffed down the toilet bowl. If the couple had been parents to a toddler, they might not have looked for an unusual explanation, but as they were the only two people living in the house and neither of them would have been foolish enough to purposely cause themselves such trouble, they were very puzzled.

Wayne and his neighbours didn't see a lot of one another during the following months, but during the Christmas season the couple invited Wayne to accept their hospitality and a holiday drink. He happily agreed to go and the three sat chatting in the couple's living-room for a time. The sound of dishes rattling in the kitchen caught Wayne off guard. He'd thought they were alone in the house.

"You must have company," he commented, pointedly looking for an explanation.

"Oh, no," came the reply. "That's just Igor. He likes to stack the dishes."

Responding to the puzzled look on their guest's face, the couple explained that Igor was their resident spirit. Although they'd never seen him, they were made very aware of his presence in their home by his mischievous acts. Igor's tricks were harmless, even childlike and indeed, the couple surmised that it must be the spirit of someone very young. Not only were they not bothered at all by Igor's presence, they often enjoyed showing him off to friends and family as a novel house pet of sorts.

As a skeptic, Wayne found their story only mildly amusing and certainly not convincing. This was, however, only his first visit to the house. Little did Wayne know that Igor had plenty of tricks left up his sleeve—more than enough to convince even the most hard-nosed doubter.

On a return visit to the haunted house, Wayne excused himself from the living-room and made his way down the hallway towards the bathroom. He noticed a large, cheerful-looking teddy bear propped up in a standing position in the hall. As he left the bathroom, he saw that the bear had fallen and he tried to prop it up in its original position. Several minutes and a great deal of frustration later, Wayne rejoined his hosts. No amount of propping was ever going to get that stuffed animal in an upright position. The bear was a rag-doll type with floppy legs that could never have supported its body. Who or what had made it stand just minutes before? "Probably Igor" was the best answer that anyone could give.

Igor also liked to redecorate. Wayne remembers seeing the basement recreation room virtually torn apart after the active spirit had made its way through it. Not only had heavy pieces of furniture been turned over, but a picture hung upside down on the wall. He didn't check the back of the picture at the time but ever since, Wayne has wondered how it would have been physically possible to "hang" in that position, given that the wire and fasteners were undoubtedly fixed to the top of the frame.

Whatever was at work in Wayne's neighbour's place was clearly gaining strength as time went on. What had once been at best a source of amusement and at worst a nuisance was now taking a toll on the quality of the couple's lives. After observing a typically Igor-like stunt, the man of the house cried out in displeasure, "Stop that, Igor!"

That simple sentence, it seemed was the turning point. As he shouted the exasperated order from his position at the top of the stairs, he felt a powerful push against his back. The force was strong enough to send him tumbling to the floor below. The couple decided that it was now time for Igor to leave.

But how could they get him to go? First they consulted the Catholic church, but they were told that the church believed that only people, not buildings or places, could be possessed. A call to the university netted no help either, only an explanation that involved "magnetic earth waves."

They were nearly ready to give up when one final and very strange incident took place. A delivery man showed up at the door with a package. By the time they realized that there was no return address on it, the courier was gone. Neither the husband nor the wife could remember what the man wore, whether he had on a uniform or not, what he looked like, or even what kind of a vehicle he was driving.

They were soon to regret their lack of attention to detail for the package the man delivered was an unsettling one. It contained a lacy black negligee, and a baroque, obscenely ornate card covered with leering cherubs. The message inside the card was in old English. Wayne remembers only one phrase from the greeting, something about "ye olde angels." And not only was the card unsigned, but there was no trademark to identify its manufacturer. If either the Hallmark company or the Carlton company had made this particular greeting card, they hadn't put their name to it.

The strange and unexpected gift filled the couple with disgust and they immediately connected the prank with Igor. Not wanting to encourage any further interaction with the power they had no under-standing of, they stuffed the negligee and grotesque card into a plastic bag and took it out to the trash. Within minutes of having done so, they rethought their actions and went to retrieve the articles. Per-haps with this added evidence they might get a more satisfying expla-nation out of the experts they'd previously consulted. And this result might in fact have been the case, but we'll never know, because Igor must have seen the plan formulating. Although mere minutes had passed since they had deposited the package in the trash, it had disap-peared completely.

By then the couple had had more than enough of living in a haunted house. They listed the place for sale and moved out not long after. In the meantime Wayne married, and although he and his new wife never heard any strange stories from any of the series of new neighbours who paraded in and out of "Igor's house," they did note that not only did the property change hands frequently, but it stood empty for long periods of time.

Apparently some spirits simply won't be chased away merely by de-termination and a positive outlook.

THE SPIRIT OF THE STATELY OLD RESIDENCE

I met Betty Harris (a pseudonym) one wonderfully cold and bright afternoon in November 1994, while doing a reading in the northwest of our province. Betty had developed something of an interest in Alberta ghosts many years ago when, as a teenager in Lethbridge, she had lived in a haunted house.

"One evening, when I was about 16, a friend [whom we shall call Jack] and I walked past a historic old house in Lethbridge," Betty began. "My friend suddenly became very agitated and said there was something about the house that bothered him immensely. He seemed very disturbed, and was relieved when we had passed by."

By coincidence, less than a year later, Betty's parents bought the stately old three-storey place as their family home. As soon as the Harrises were unpacked and settled in, Betty invited Jack over for a visit. The boy's reaction to being inside the house was considerably more bizarre than the discomfort he had felt the year before when he and Betty had walked past it.

As the teens toured first the main floor and then the second storey of the house, Jack remained composed. It wasn't until he tried to climb the staircase leading to the home's third storey that everything changed.

"He was physically unable to mount the stairs leading to the third storey. I watched as he grasped the banister, lifted his foot to the first step, and then strained against some invisible force that prevented him from advancing," Betty recalled. "The same held true for descending the basement stairs."

Showing that she had a very practical nature, even as a teenager, Betty added, "I must confess I thought it was just theatrics on his part." She and Jack set the incident as far aside as they could and continued to enjoy their friendship.

There is perhaps no place as important to teenage girls as their bedrooms. The privacy and security provided by a girl's bedroom can create a sanctuary in an often troubled world. Betty explained that her bedroom in the family's new home was on the second floor of the house and overlooked the front yard.

"Right after we moved in, I noticed that as I lay on it, my bed would occasionally begin to gently shake back and forth. I was puzzled and tried to find an explanation. Was there traffic going by outside? Were the washer and dryer, located on the same level [of the house] running and causing the floor and bed to vibrate? Was the furnace causing the house to shudder as it switched on and off? None of these explanations panned out. I asked my parents, whose bedroom was just across the hall, but they hadn't noticed anything and passed the whole thing off," Betty remembered.

Eventually Betty gave up looking for an explanation for her swaying bed and just accepted it as a quirky addition to her life. "It didn't frighten me. It was very gentle and benign. If I woke up in the night and my bed was shaking, it would feel more like being rocked back to sleep than anything else," she said.

On one occasion, however, the shaking turned out to have a definite, different purpose.

"One night my boyfriend [not Jack] and I had a disagreement. He became upset and left, saying that nobody understood him. I had no idea just how upset he was until, later that night, I was jolted out of my sleep by a violently shaking bed. It had never shaken with such force before. At first I thought, 'Oh, it's just the bed shaking,' and I rolled over and tried to go back to sleep. I kept getting this nagging feeling that I should go to the window," Betty explained. "Finally, in exasperation, I thought I'd just get up and go to the window and get it out of my system."

To this day, Betty is grateful for having acted on that impulse.

"As I peered out the window, I made out a shape huddled on the front lawn. It was my boyfriend. He had slashed his wrists and was lying in a pool of blood. If my bed shaking hadn't wakened me, and if I hadn't obeyed the urge to go to the window, he would have died a very short time later, out there on the lawn."

Clearly, whatever force was at work in that historic old mansion knew that, without intervention, a tragedy would have occurred.

Although the man whose life was saved and Betty are no longer in touch with one another, the incident remains an understandably vivid memory for the woman. No wonder she ventured out that November afternoon in 1994 to hear me reading about other people's experiences in our spirit-filled province.

THE LITTLE
BOY AND THE LADY

Many of the dramas that make up our lives are played out in our homes. If the trauma is forceful enough, something of a psychic imprint can remain long after the event itself is over and even, for the most part, forgotten about. Considering this effect, it should be no surprise that we have so many haunted houses. In fact, it's probably only surprising that we don't have more. The following story about a house in Islay, near Lloydminster, certainly falls into the justifiably haunted category.

By the late 1980s, the Alberta Wheat Pool was suspending the practice of providing housing for its employees. One by one it was selling off the many houses it owned in the small towns that dot Alberta's landscape. One of those dwellings was a two-storey place with a tragic recent history. Apparently a former Wheat Pool employee murdered his wife in the company house.

Some time later, a young couple with a three-year-old boy bought the house. At first, when the youngster began to tell his parents about the lady upstairs, they paid very little attention to his stories, presuming they were only hearing the fruits of a child's fertile imagination.

"He said she was nice and came to him often," according to the woman who relayed the story to me. The child was so accepting of his visitor that his mother now realizes that she might never have known about her son's strange companion if it hadn't been for a concern of the child's. He apparently could not understand what the woman was saying to him and that frustrated the child.

The child may have been totally accepting of his invisible visitor, but his mother was understandably frightened by the implications of the situation. She shared that discomfort with a few friends. They frequently reported seeing an apparition at a window on the second storey. Today, some twenty years later, she does wonder if there was an element of teasing in their stories, but even if that were so, it wouldn't have explained her little boy's experiences.

THE EVIL HOUSE IN IRMA

This ghost story travelled a long way to be included here. The incident occurred in Irma, near Wainwright, but was sent to me from a man in Alexander, Manitoba. He had been listening to a radio talk show from Brandon on which I was a guest. This well-travelled tale is one of the most frightening and dramatic I've ever been told.

In 1976, Shane Bates and his wife were young parents living in Virden, Manitoba.

"I was in the construction business and was called by a friend [in Alberta] to come out that way because there was lots of work available," Shane said.

The family moved to Alberta, but for the first month stayed with their friends, rather than getting their own place right away.

"Then we decided to rent a house and stay at least until the work boom died away. We decided to rent a small house in Irma mainly because it was close to Wainwright and the rent was unusually cheap. I think they were asking about $100 a month," Shane remembered. He noted that the figure compared very favourably to other rents in the area, which generally ran about $250 to $350 per month.

Saving money was important to the young couple because, although still just in their twenties, they had a family of four children in addition to the family dog, a chihuahua.

"We were due to move into the house on the first of August 1976. The local real estate company handling the rental gave us permission to move in the last week of July," observed the husband. "My wife and I decided to spend the first night without the children as we were painting inside the house. We left our children with our friends in Wainwright."

They did, however, take the family pet with them.

"The dog was a very brave and loyal dog, even though he only weighed about 10 pounds," Shane foreshadowed cryptically.

"We hadn't moved any furniture in yet, so we were going to sleep on air mattresses on the floor," Shane went on. "Nothing unusual had been noticed all day while we were cleaning and painting. About 10 o'clock we decided to lay down for the night. As we laid there for a short while I was aware of voices from somewhere. It sounded like several people in low conversation. We couldn't understand the words but were aware of the drone of talking and the odd sounds of laughter."

Animals often seem to have a more accurate sense of a paranormal presence than humans do and this was certainly the case in this haunted house. "The dog began to bark and whine and shiver," Shane noted. "He ran to the basement and barked loudly while trembling and howling like I never heard him do before. I got up and looked out the windows…all was dark and no one was around."

Confused and concerned, Shane decided to investigate further. "When I opened the door to the basement, the dog yelped and ran to my wife in bed. I closed the basement door. The dog was now letting out a long, mournful howl, which was eerie in itself."

Shane took the time to explain that this sort of behaviour was completely out of character for the family pet. "This dog, which would normally attack a 150 pound [68 kilogram] German shepherd, was reduced to a shaking, whining lump under the blankets. I called to the dog to come and...normally he would have leapt up barking and growling." This time, however, the dog would not leave the safety it felt it had found huddled in the bedding beside Shane's wife.

"My wife and I were now hearing knocking sounds on [the] walls and [the] floor. I went to [the] outside door and looked, but there was no sign of anybody. Suddenly the banging got louder, in fact [my wife] sprung from her mattress as a very loud bang struck directly beneath her from below." The whole scenario had become utterly terrifying.

"The voices were louder now but still not audible, although they sounded angry. The banging increased in volume and amount. We could actually feel the vibrations of the blows through the floor." Not surprisingly, Shane added, "My wife and I were suddenly overcome by a tremendous fear. We were no longer curious or puzzled. We were now terrified."

Shane reached down and grabbed his very last bit of courage.

"In a last effort of bravery, I threw open the basement door and yelled, 'Who are you? What do you want?' The door slammed shut with such force the bang of the impact was ear-piercing. The dog had now attempted to exit by diving at a window and was urinating everywhere. The feeling of dread and danger was overwhelming. I yelled to my wife...'Come on! Now!' I raced to the outside door and we left. The dog beat us to the door. We piled into the car and got away. It was a very long time—hours—before we calmed down."

The Bates family knew that there was no way they could ever call that haunted house home and so they went about cancelling the arrangements they'd made. "The next day I called the real estate company and told them we decided not to take the house," Shane recounted. "They were very calm and promised to return our rent."

Perhaps reinforced by the company's response, Shane questioned the rental agent as discreetly as he could. He asked if there'd ever been reports of unusual happenings from previous tenants. "The lady seemed very guarded about her answer, but said a lot of people had come and gone through the house over the last several years. Most didn't stay more than a month," he remembered her revealing.

The terror-filled evening cost the Bates family some sheets and blan-kets. "I didn't return for our bedding. I just couldn't muster enough courage to go in that house again."

Now, twenty years later, the dreadful experience is still fresh in Shane Bates's mind and it is still just as confusing. "To this day, I don't know what caused the commotion but I know what I heard and so does my wife. Whatever it was didn't want us there," he noted.

A sad postscript to this story attests to the horrors those two young people and their little dog suffered. As Shane recalled, "The dog re-acted slightly differently than us. It seemed as soon as we left that house, the dog returned to normal. In fact, that brave little dog was killed in a fight with a dog [that] outweighed him by 100 pounds about a year after his experience in '76."

The humans, however, took longer to recover from the experience. "I am trembling just recalling that night," Shane readily admitted.

ACTIVE APPARITION STAYS BEHIND

In the early 1980s, the Hlady family bought a duplex bungalow in the Calder area of Edmonton.

"Our daughters' friends told them there'd been a murder in the house," explained Nancy Hlady. "I have no way of knowing whether that's true or not. The place had been empty for some time when we bought it."

Empty, that is except for an alarming presence.

Initially, the family had no indication that their new home was haunted. Then their daughter, Jill, awoke one night to see the image of a man at the end of her bed. He held a knife. The terrified youngster screamed at the vision to leave but it remained. Finally, in a panic, Jill fled from the room to the safety of her parents' bedroom.

The next instance took place when Jill's older sister, Shelly, was alone in the house. She was doing laundry, her mind a million miles away, when she suddenly felt she was not alone. Startled, Shelly looked up quickly and saw a figure of a man wearing a cloak. She stared, horrified, for what she estimates to have been thirty seconds. Then the apparition vanished. This vision recurred. The second time as well, though it left as quickly as it had appeared, Shelly was able to recognize its appearance from the first visit.

Teenage girls sometimes have vivid imaginations, and it might be tempting to write both experiences off as adolescence-inspired fantasies. This haunted-house story, however, will not be so easily pigeon-holed, for the girls' parents also had encounters with the presence in their home.

"We built the master bedroom downstairs," explained Ron. "One time Nancy went down there and all the lights in our bedroom were flashing on and off. And many times I'd be sitting downstairs in the family room watching television and I'd suddenly smell perfume or peanut butter or something else. That happened many, many times."

In spite of these ghostly goings-on, the Hladys lived in the haunted house for nearly ten years. When they finally sold the place, they wondered if whatever they'd been unwillingly sharing their lives with might follow them. Happily, the unpleasant presence apparently decided not to leave the community of Calder.

FAMILY FEARS
IN ISOLATION

The following is one of the most poignant stories I've ever received. Brenda's story of sharing her tumultuous teen years with a ghost seemed to have exploded onto the notepaper. Despite the cathartic and dramatic essence to the letter, Brenda stated flatly that there's "so much more...so many things happened...too many."

In February 1994, during an interview in Brenda's home, I listened intently as she recalled one dreadful instance after another. Undoubtedly, the saddest aspect of this family's experience is that all of its members suffered in silent isolation, thinking that they were alone in feeling the presence and that the others would think them mad if they tried to explain. This secrecy existed until first Brenda and then other members of her family read my earlier book. The similarities between their experiences and those recorded in that book gave each one enough self-assurance so that at last they were comfortable confiding in one another. While this opening up didn't undo the damage caused by the stress of living with a ghost for years, it at least broke down the barriers to communication among those involved.

In the late 1960s, the family lived in the Kingsland area of Calgary in a house that had been moved from Okotoks. Brenda's brother researched the building's history and learned that it dated back to the turn of the century. He also discovered that a man had hanged himself in the house.

Brenda explained that everyone in the family hated one particular bedroom of this house. Unfortunately, someone had to sleep there and it was assigned to Brenda.

"I would lie in bed and listen to strange noises," Brenda began. "It sounded to me like birds fluttering around in the attic, but they seemed to be calling my name. I would talk to whatever it was and tell my troubles to it. My brother's told me since that what I heard was probably the ghosts."

By the mid-1970s, the family moved again, this time to Allen Crescent in southeast Calgary. Not long after the family had vacated the old house, workers demolished it to make room for new construction. It was then that the strange and uncomfortable occurrences that would torment the family for years began in the new house. They now presume that the presence accompanied them to their new home before the old one was destroyed.

Brenda's father, William, reports that the family dog seemed affected right from the beginning. Unless someone carried it, the animal would never go downstairs; instead, the dog stood at the top of the stairs looking down into the basement, whimpering. Occasionally they'd watch the fur on the dog's neck stand up as he reacted in terror to some unseen entity.

William watched the frightened animal with great sympathy because he too felt terribly uncomfortable whenever he went downstairs. The uneasy feeling of being watched never left the man while he worked in the basement. One day something in a corner near his work bench caught the man's eye. Glancing over quickly, he found himself staring into a mist that then disappeared as he watched.

Brenda's mother, Dianne, dreaded doing laundry, not for the work involved but because it meant she'd have to be down in the basement. Like her husband, Dianne felt a presence in that area of the house. One particular day as the woman stood facing the washing machine, she knew a large, husky man stood behind her, looking down and watching her. Although jolted by the sensation, she remained calm. She didn't feel threatened by the presence—she felt that it was harmless, that it was only curious.

The spirit proved Dianne's assessment to be right on a number of occasions. It seemed endlessly fascinated with both the washer and the dryer. He made a habit of turning them on and off when no one else was anywhere near the machines.

Early adolescence is often a difficult time not only for those going through it themselves, but also for their parents and siblings. Ghosts, however, find these hormone-infused youngsters extremely attractive. Brenda's sister, Lynn, explains that she had just entered her teens when the family moved from the house in Kingsland.

"I didn't pay that much attention to what was going on in the [new] house," the woman recalled. Nevertheless, "even though I was distracted with a first boyfriend and really involved with my friends, [I] couldn't help but feel a strangeness in the house, especially in the basement. There was always the sense of someone or something behind me, especially [in the basement] if my back was turned to the staircase. I felt it was strongest from underneath the staircase, but there was a strong presence on that whole side of the basement. I couldn't get back upstairs fast enough," Lynn added.

With the exception of the basement, Lynn reported feeling safe in the house, except in her brother's bedroom, most particularly near the closet. Coincidentally, that closet stood directly over the area where the washer and dryer were kept in the basement below.

When relatives came to stay, Lynn gave up her bedroom and slept downstairs. "With the excitement of having cousins stay with us, I didn't pay much thought to having to sleep in the basement. My brother also moved downstairs. He told me I sat up in bed one night and called to him. My eyes were wide open. I appeared to be awake. He asked me what was wrong and I said, 'Nothing, it's okay.' then I slid back down. I have absolutely no memory of [the event]."

Oddly, the visitor assigned to sleep in Lynn's room, the only room in the house where Lynn felt entirely safe, experienced disturbing nightmares there during his visit.

"While sleeping in my room he came running into the living-room saying there was a spider on his arm. He was trying to shake it off. To me it seems that the house was not pleased with the sleeping arrangements and wanted things back to normal. The company wasn't welcome. The house seemed mad, tense," Lynn explained.

Now, nearly twenty years later, Lynn finds that the general layout of the house comes to mind easily, but that she has no recollection of certain areas in the basement. Lynn explained that the years of living with an unseen presence have taken a permanent toll on her. "I still have a great fear of basements," she admitted, and then added a dramatic postscript to her narrative: "I will always think of [the house on] Allen Crescent. Not only the house we lived in but the house that lived around and along with us."

Listening to Brenda and Lynn tell of the family's experiences in the haunted house that the family called home, the terror that Brenda felt as a child clearly remains, even though she is now a grown woman with an adolescent daughter of her own.

"There was a sense of someone moving along beside you when you were on the stairs," Brenda recalled. "You never lost the feeling that someone was watching you. I knew it was a man. I could even tell he was tall and muscular. It stared at me. Each one of us thought we were going crazy. One night the washer and dryer were going on and off by themselves and I could feel someone behind me. I turned around slowly. I saw a shadow on the floor, but [there was] nothing there to cast it," she recalled. "Everyone hated one particular corner of the basement" between the dryer and the freezer.

Although the family dog clearly disliked whatever was in the basement of the house, it allowed Brenda to carry it downstairs to her bedroom. One Christmas Eve, the dog refused to go downstairs but stood whimpering and barking at the top of the stairs.

"You could tell that the presence was there," Brenda remembered. "The dog would run."

Eventually the animal calmed down enough to allow Brenda to take it downstairs and to bed. In the morning the youngster awoke to the sound of her dog growling. She looked in the direction of the dog's attention and saw a mysterious globe of light on the wall.

"It didn't illuminate," the woman struggled to explain. "It was just there. When I got up to investigate, it was gone."

With a deep breath, Brenda continued. "You could hear [the man's spirit] walking downstairs as though it had heavy work boots on. He had broad shoulders."

When Brenda realized that this spirit might be the presence she'd heard from the attic of the old house, she spoke to the ghost. "You're here, aren't you?" she asked it, but got no reply.

Living with the feeling of being constantly watched never left Brenda, and it made her extremely self-conscious and uncomfortable. "It made me feel so dirty," she explained. "I never had any privacy. It watched me get undressed and take a bath. Then it would do things to me like take my birth control pills and put them under the bed or under the pillow. One night as I lay in bed, I felt my hair being touched and tugged. I could feel the presence and it felt like it was saying 'No.' I finally turned my head. There was no one there but there was an impression as though someone had been sitting on the bed."

When all these experiences became too much for the teenager to bear, she would yell at the ghost.

"It didn't speak. The communication was mind-to-mind. I would get a 'HA, HA, HA' reaction."

It's not much of a surprise that these experiences have had a lasting influence on Brenda. "I won't live in a place with a basement," she stated simply. As I looked around, I only then noticed that the four-plex where she lived with her husband and daughter was a bilevel building and therefore indeed had no basement.

As I left the interview, I thanked the family, not only for their hospitality that afternoon, but also for sharing their painful tale so candidly. They, in turn, thanked me for having created the catalyst (my previous book of ghost stories) that had finally released all their family members from their dreadful secret.

HAUNTED IN HIGH LEVEL

Some stories took amazingly indirect routes to my mailbox and the following tale certainly falls into that category. I called the Galt Museum in Lethbridge in an attempt to get the story of a haunted house in Fort Macleod...and ended up with a ghost story from High Level, at virtually the opposite corner of the province.

The people involved in the story consist of the wife and mother, Mellina; her husband, Calvin; their two young sons, Kaelin and Stefan; and their boarder, Glen. The five moved into the rented farmhouse about 35 kilometres east of the town of High Level on October 1, 1992. The building was about thirty years old at the time and was about 1 kilometre away from the nearest neighbour.

The strange experiences began within the first month. As Calvin and Glen stood at the entrance to the kitchen, a bottle of liquid detergent on the counter caught their eye. It rocked back and forth so vigorously that it should have fallen on its side. The two men watched in silence until the phenomenon stopped of its own accord. When the bottle stood still again, Glen jokingly suggested the house might be haunted and then the men continued the interrupted conversation.

Several weeks later, Calvin and Mellina stayed up later than usual to enjoy each other's company. Throughout the evening, the power flickered off and on for no apparent reason. Shortly after the couple finally turned in for the night, they heard the distinctive sound of a car door slamming two or three times. As Glen had been out for the evening, Calvin assumed that their boarder had returned home. He got out of bed to open the door for the man and stared in disbelief at the empty yard.

Shaken, he returned to bed. As the two settled back to try to sleep, they heard footsteps coming from the attic, followed by a loud crash.

"We were both quite frightened," Mellina remembered.

Moments later they heard a loud crash, but neither Calvin nor Mellina could tell which part of the house the sound came from. At this point, eighteen-month-old Stefan woke up crying inconsolably. His parents knew something unusual had disturbed their son because he had been sleeping soundly through the night since infancy.

To the couple's dismay, that incident broke the child's previously sound sleeping pattern. They discovered that if they put Stefan to bed in that particular room where he had been placed, he wouldn't sleep through the night. Within months, they began calling that room "the ghost room" and had all but stopped using it. In addition to interrupted sleep, Mellina noted that "this bedroom was always cold, or at least colder than every other room in the house."

One evening, long after putting her sons to bed, Mellina sat reading in the living-room. Neither Calvin nor Glen was home at the time. Mellina watched in horror as the door to an unoccupied bedroom slowly opened and closed several times over the period of a few minutes.

This last incident triggered the end of Mellina's tolerance and unquestioning acceptance of the strange occurrences in her home. "We knew of a woman who lived a couple of hours away who could sense ghosts and how they felt and if they were good or evil. We asked her to come to the house and she did. She walked through the whole house and said she most definitely felt a presence."

This presence, the woman told them, was in the bedroom they'd stopped using, the one they called the ghost room.

"She said she felt the ghost was very sad and did not mean us any harm. Before her visit, Calvin and I were talking of moving out. This woman said that the ghost trusted us and was upset that we were thinking of leaving. It wanted to make itself known to us," Mellina reported.

The spirit's attention-getting behaviours didn't end there. One afternoon, shortly after Mellina tucked the boys in for their afternoon nap, she heard someone calling "Mommy." She checked on the children immediately because, although the voice seemed to come from the room where Stefan lay sleeping, the child could only say "Mama" and had not yet mastered "Mommy." However, both children lay quietly asleep.

Mellina explained that she heard "Mommy" herself "a few times," and that it "happened twice for Calvin when I was not home."

Mellina and her family stayed surprisingly calm during these incidents and approached the occurrences with an admirably pragmatic attitude.

What Mellina referred to as a "major incident" would have had lesser souls calling for the moving truck. She began to hear banging noises at night. The sounds emanated from the wall connecting with the ghost room. "I would hear the banging, which sounded like a steady knocking sound. I would wake Calvin up and the noises would immediately stop. After Calvin fell asleep again, the knocking would begin again. Each time I woke Calvin, the noise would stop. At some point Stefan would wake up, crying hysterically. Other noises from this wall were tapping and vibrating sounds. Since Stefan's crib was up against this wall we thought maybe Stefan, as he moved in his sleep, caused the banging. We even tested it out by banging the crib against the wall while one of us was in our bedroom but there was no noticeable noise. One day as I was standing in that bedroom [the ghost room] I noticed the child-sized wooden rocking chair next to the crib.

I started rocking it with my hand. It banged against the wall and produced the exact same noise that we [had] heard in the night."

After Mellina and Calvin moved Stefan from this room, they never heard the banging again.

Mellina knew that the previous tenant (a man) of the house practised strange religious customs involving the devil and evil. The lady who had sensed the spirit in their house had told the family that they must never let this man back into their house. "One day the man showed up and preached his religion to me for nearly an hour on my front step. I did not let him enter the house. He mentioned to me that what was in the house was definitely the devil trying to possess our souls. Needless to say we dismissed and disregarded his ideas.

"That night, as I was putting Stefan to bed, something strange happened. The room was dark. I was sitting on the floor next to the crib, singing, when a loud hissing noise filled the room. I was terrified. I grabbed Stefan, put on the light and ran out of the room. The ghost was obviously upset that I had allowed the religious man even near the house. [I heard that the man's] family claims they had no [spooky] incidents or experiences happen to them while they lived in the house for two years."

That spring, the family held a joint birthday party for their sons, Kaelin and Stefan. Happy chaos reined throughout the house that day. By evening, toys lay scattered around, including a large metal toy tractor in the laundry room. On top of the tractor lay a purple toy saw.

Mellina's sister and family were visiting and decided to stay the night. The only bedroom available was the one the family had stopped using, the ghost room. In the middle of the night, Mellina's sister heard a loud crash.

"She got up thinking one of the kids woke up. She checked all the kids, but they were all asleep. She walked into the laundry room and noticed the tractor was turned upside down, with the purple saw underneath it. Everyone else was sleeping at the time," Mellina remarked.

The family avoided using that bedroom whenever possible, but occasionally it became necessary to use it. When Mellina tried to put

Kaelin, her four-year-old son, to bed in the ghost room, he seemed unable to relax. Mellina lay beside him to help the child fall asleep, but to no avail.

"Kaelin lay on his back very stiffly right up against me. I asked him to move over and he refused. He was staring towards the ceiling. He said he heard a noise and claimed he saw something spinning," Mellina recalled. "My husband and I never said anything in front of the kids about what was happening in the house," she admitted.

That night Kaelin relaxed only after Mellina moved him to another area of the house.

We know that animals often sense paranormal presences far more accurately than humans do. The actions of the family's cats may have been evidence that they sensed something unusual. The first time the oldest cat went into the ghost room, the animal scurried frantically around the room, pausing only to paw at the floor. Oddly, the room later became the cat's favourite—the room of choice for its catnaps.

When the family brought a second cat home, this younger animal reacted exactly as the other cat had when it approached the ghost room for the first time. Afterwards, it too preferred to sleep in that room. The younger cat occasionally perked up its ears as though it heard something and scurried into its favourite room. Both cats loved to stare into the closet of that bedroom even though, to the human eye the closet appeared to be empty.

Whatever possessed the house made itself known to Mellina's mother one evening as she babysat her grandsons. She heard a car door slam and prepared to greet her daughter and son-in-law. But they weren't home yet and there was no vehicle in the yard.

The family eventually accepted nightly banging and crashing sounds and even the sounds of footsteps from the attic as normal for that house—nevertheless they routinely checked for a source but never found one.

Even after little Stefan had been given a new bedroom, he continued to be disturbed by the ghost room. One night he woke up crying. "Baby," the child informed his mother. He pointed across the hall to his old bedroom and announced, "That one."

The family moved from the house on September 30, 1993, and apparently left the spirit behind. The memories of living in a haunted house, however, will likely never leave them.

HAUNTED APARTMENT TO LET

Donna and John, who have asked that their last name not be used, live in Edmonton with their four children. Donna owns a busy retail outlet and John is engaged in a successful professional practice. These are active, intelligent people, well aware of life's realities and not given to flights of fancy.

My family has known John on a casual but ongoing basis for the better part of twenty years. One day he surprised me with the comment, "My wife wants you to call her." Fortunately, he quickly added the rider, "She has a ghost story for you."

I did call Donna the next day and she certainly did have a ghost story for me – one of the most dramatic I've ever heard.

In 1991, when Donna decided to expand her Edmonton business, she chose a location in the resort town of Banff. Because operating this store would mean long and tiring periods away from home, Donna rented a large two-storey apartment. To give me an idea of the size of the suite, Donna explained, "It was the top of a whole building—the place slept twelve."

Donna's background is in health care and so it's not surprising that the first part of settling into her home-away-from-home involved cleaning the apartment thoroughly. With that chore accomplished, she began to stay in the Banff apartment one day a week. Because the place was so big, and her stays there so limited, Donna rented one of the downstairs bedrooms to a business associate. Donna retained a large upstairs bedroom. The first few months passed uneventfully. Then, without warning, the first in a long list of strange and frightening events occurred.

"I began to hear noises coming from the roof," she explained. "It sounded like a team of guys stomping and dragging chains across the gravel roof."

Although the noise disturbed her, Donna ignored it as best she could until one afternoon when her husband, John, accompanied her on the trip from Edmonton to Banff. They arrived tired from their long drive and lay down to have a nap. Before Donna could drift off to sleep, the noises on the roof began once again. Wanting to explain that this cacophony was a regular disruption during her stays in Banff, Donna turned to John. More than a little surprised, Donna stared at her husband lying beside her—he was fast asleep, apparently oblivious to the racket going on overhead. As the next few months were to disclose, this was the first in a series of incidents that only Donna seemed to be attuned to.

Even with one full-time tenant and Donna's weekly visits, the apartment in Banff was still very much under-utilized and so when her store manager needed a place to live, Donna arranged for the woman to take one of the empty bedrooms. This bedroom was, like Donna's, also on the second floor, and so right below the roof, but the manager never complained of the noises that had disturbed Donna. Donna seemed to be the only one hearing the racket, and even her experiences with the noises were limited. "I only heard the chains on the roof if I tried to sleep," she acknowledged, before adding, "Then came the smell."

Foul, intense odours that pervade an area for varying durations are frequently associated with a haunted place. Knowing that the place was scrupulously clean, Donna was puzzled and annoyed, with this malodorous addition to her apartment. Worse, as with the noises from the roof, Donna seemed to be the only one aware of the smell.

"I used potpourri to combat it, but that didn't solve the problem," she recalled. She remembered that the foul smell was so strong and had such a sudden onset that it seemed to her that "instantly you were in the middle of it."

Finally, her colleague, the store manager, also became aware of the foul odour, which Donna described as a stench like a combination of rotten meat and feces. The smell seemed to be concentrated in another big bedroom and the two women wondered if possibly the vents in the room were bringing in the hideous odour from another part of the building. They checked out this possibility and were disturbed to find that their theory was incorrect.

So far whoever or whatever Donna was unwittingly sharing her apartment with had tried sound and smell to get her attention. The next sense the spirit appealed to was sight. Donna set up the scenario for me by describing the design of the kitchen. Exterior light to that room was provided by a skylight in the ceiling and the kitchen doors were accented with gold-coloured glass.

"I arrived [at the apartment] one night about 8," she recalled. "It was a very black night. [As seen from outside,] the windows were all aglow with gold, as if my bedroom lights were on and shining through the gold glass."

This phenomenon surprised and concerned Donna, because she'd expected the apartment to be empty when she arrived. Understandably nervous, the woman entered the building making as much noise as possible. She half expected to scare off an intruder but the place was as empty as she'd expected it to be. Empty of people that is, but filled with the foul odour. By the time she reached the kitchen, the golden glowing light she seen from the outside had disappeared.

On another occasion, Donna and John had invited a group of their friends for a ski weekend. Donna was the first one awake in the morning. She tidied the place up a bit and plugged in the coffee urns for their inevitable use. As she walked through the apartment, she was mortified to realize that the now-familiar stench saturated the air yet again. She knew the place was clean. She also knew that her friends would be astonished by such an odour in one of her homes. After all, these people knew Donna and John well. They knew Donna's obsession with cleanliness—some had even dubbed her Mrs Clean. But here she was, offering hospitality to friends when there was obviously filth somewhere in the place. Nothing but filth could account for a stench this rancid. The smell was throughout the whole place but seemed to be concentrated under the staircase, right where the fax machine sat.

Oddly, when her guests arose a little while later, no one commented on anything out of the ordinary. They seemed completely unaware of any sort of a smell. As puzzled as she was relieved, Donna set about enjoying her weekend of camaraderie and skiing.

Several months later, Donna was asleep in her home in Edmonton. She began to dream of the place in Banff and the horrid smell she so often had to endure when she stayed there. In her dream she was determined to track down the cause of the stench.

"I opened my tenant's bedroom door. A sheet of strong odour hit me," she described. "It was so strong my eyes were watering. Then, for the first time, I'm thinking 'It's a body.'"

In her nightmare, Donna made her way through the man's room. "The end of the bedroom leads to an open area. The smell was even stronger there," she recalled.

Swinging open the door to the en-suite bathroom, she watched as her nightmare unraveled a horrific scene to her. "The door hit a bloated body. I saw it through the mirror above the vanity. The body burst and splattered all over the wall. I backed out of the room and telephoned the guy who rented the room. I asked him, 'Did you give anyone the key?' He said he hadn't. I hung up and called the police."

In Donna's dream, the police arrived to find her standing, frozen and mute, pointing to the bedroom door.

At last Donna was released from her terror by the return of consciousness. "I woke up panting from the terror," she recalled. "I looked at the clock radio and it was 2:49 [AM]."

Now whatever inhabited her Banff home was making itself felt even when Donna was hundreds of kilometres away. What she didn't know at the time was that she was sharing the frightening experience with her friend Mary, who was staying in the Banff apartment. Mary too awoke in terror at 2:49 AM that same night. She had been fast asleep when she felt a hand on her face. She awoke to find herself alone in the darkened room. The only light came from the luminous dial of the clock radio, indicating that it was 2:49.

Perhaps the worst aspect of the two terrifying experiences was that despite their deep and long-standing friendship, both women were so shaken by their experiences that they could not bring themselves to discuss the strange events for a long time. It was many months later that they finally were able to confide in one another and at least find some sort of solace in the fact that both had had related experiences.

Mary circumvented the possibility of ever being exposed to that dark terror again by never staying another night in her friend's haunted apartment. For Donna, however, that was not an option and so her experiences of terror continued.

On another trip to the mountain town, Donna was alone in the apartment. She was in bed in the large room that she usually used. In addition to the queen-size bed where Donna lay, there were bunk-beds and a single bed. As she lay in the dark trying to drop off to sleep, the woman felt a presence in the room. She turned on the light. There was nothing there, at least that she could see. She moved to the middle of her bed. Neither the light nor the move helped.

"I had a feeling of impending doom. I moved to my daughter's single bed. I shoved it up against the wall," said Donna, remembering her attempts to protect herself from an unseen evil. Eventually the feeling lessened and disappeared. During that experience there was no rancid stench.

Donna's long-suffering nature had coped with nearly enough by now. Unfortunately for Donna, the presence wasn't through. She went on to explain, "It shoved me on the shoulder. I was in the dressing area [of the main bedroom], walking towards the bathroom, and someone shoved me. It was a sharp push."

The feeling of being shoved is an unpleasant experience at any time, but certainly decidedly worse when you know for a fact, as Donna did, that you are the only person in the room.

Living, even part-time, in a place that is haunted by something so clearly evil had taken its toll. Donna made some inquiries of locals about the history of the building that housed this strange suite.

"It was a bad story. There'd been a little house on the land before. An old alcoholic lived there with his son. The man died in the house. I think it burned down," she recalled having learned.

That information triggered Donna's memory of her horrible nightmare about finding the body. "I think the body [in the dream] had its hands tied behind its back. Someone's got to investigate," she concluded.

Would Donna herself take on the research? "No. I became so afraid that I got rid of the condo."

And so, somewhere in the town of Banff, is there still an unavenged murder victim trying to draw attention to his unnatural end, or has the force exhausted itself by now and the man's spirit gone on to its eternal rest? Perhaps someone reading this account will be able to answer that question.

RANCHER STAYS ON AFTER DEATH

"Tell her I'm not a crackpot," Katrina Diebel-Logan protested when she called David Gell, who at that time was the host of CBC radio's *Saturday Side Up* program. Katrina was responding to an interview between David and me that had aired earlier that day. The ever-courteous Mr Gell smiled at her comment and then passed Katrina's name and phone number along to me. By now he was used to having listeners phone him after they'd heard our on-air discussions. When those listeners had a ghost story of their own to tell, they often buttressed their comments with vindications of their sanity.

When I returned Katrina's call later that day, I was delighted to find out for myself that she was certainly not a crackpot, but a very down-to-earth, personable woman. Even better, she certainly had a story to tell—a ghost story—for Katrina Diebel-Logan was raised on a haunted ranch not far from Black Diamond, south of Calgary.

"My grandmother lived on that ranch for forty years," she began by way of an introduction to her tale.

Her grandparents came from Unity, Saskatchewan, to work for a rancher named Ed Marsten. The man had no children and as the years went by, he struck a deal with the couple. "Keep living and working on the ranch with me the same as always, but buy me out over the years," Ed had suggested to Katrina's grandfather.

The couple was delighted with the idea and honoured that their employer apparently thought so much of them. The bargain was struck immediately and the arrangement worked very well for a time. Katrina's grandparents built a house for themselves on the property near Marsten's house and they worked the ranch as though it was their own. Had it not been for a tragedy, the trio's original plan would no doubt have gone smoothly. As it was, however, death came to Marsten not only prematurely but violently. Worse still, police charged Katrina's grandfather with the man's murder.

Katrina explained that in the late 1940s there was a fire in the main ranch house. Mr Marsten was killed in the blaze. When an autopsy was conducted to determine the cause of the man's death, the coroner found a bullet lodged in his brain. Katrina's grandfather's financial interest in the ranch was seen as a possible motive for murder and, as he was certainly nearby when the death occurred, he was the prime suspect. The police surmised that he had shot the old man and then set the house on fire to make the death look accidental.

Fortunately for Katrina's innocent grandfather, further investigation determined that Marsten had been sitting on a package of 22-gauge shells when the house fire started and the heat from the blaze had exploded the bullets. Apparently at least one of the bullets traveled through the man's body, and came to rest buried in his brain. The murder charge was dropped immediately and the ranch-hand's name was cleared. He and his wife, Katrina's grandmother, took over ownership of the ranch. Not long after taking over, the couple began to notice odd occurrences around the ranch.

"A strong wind prevailed across the ranch," Katrina remembered. "One day the top for my grandmother's roaster was missing."

This disappearance in itself was rather peculiar, but the fact that it was not found inside the house added a further dimension of intrigue to the mystery. Of course, there was always the chance that the lid had been left on the verandah and had been blown away by the strong winds southern Alberta is noted for. Unfortunately for skeptics, that theory won't work in this case, because the roasting pan lid was found lying on the ground a good distance from the house. Even assuming that for some reason the lid had been left out on the porch and been caught by the wind, it should've been found on the other side of the property, not where it was. The metal lid couldn't possibly have travelled against such a strong and steady wind on its own.

Katrina's grandmother reported that although she was somewhat puzzled by the occurrence, she wasn't completely surprised. She'd sensed old Ed Marsten's presence in and around the ranch house as surely as if the fatal fire had never happened.

Her husband was the next to become aware of the dead man's return to his beloved ranch. For years, Katrina's grandfather would spend at least a portion of his evenings in the barn repairing equipment needed for ranch operations the next day. When he was finished, he'd turn off the lights in the old wooden building and head back to the house. It was his habit to turn and take a last glance over the property before climbing the verandah stairs and going into the house for the night. After Marsten's death, this simple pattern developed an unnerving twist: the lights inside the barn, which the man had just turned off, would often be shining brightly.

At first, of course, the man presumed that he'd neglected to turn the switch off and so he made a special effort to make sure that there were no lights lit in the barn before he headed back to the house. Despite this double check, a warm and cheery glow from the windows in the barn often met his gaze when he glanced that way after reaching the ranch-house porch. It didn't take too many of these incidents for the man to agree with his wife's opinion that their former employer was still with them.

Ed Marsten is apparently not a shy ghost nor one who gives up easily. When Katrina's grandparents sold the ranch many years ago, they wondered whether the original owner would follow them or stay with his ranch. Ed answered their question by making himself known to the new owners.

Like Katrina's grandparents, the new owners and the people they have working for them frequently hear someone walking across the verandah. They've learned by now that when they hear footsteps it doesn't necessarily mean that someone will be coming into the house—not someone they'll be able to see, anyway.

The ghost has never caused any serious trouble, although some of his pranks are undeniably annoying. For instance, working in the vegetable garden with a pitchfork seems to be an invitation for Ed's ghost to start playing tricks. He may let you work undisturbed, but you can be sure that the only place you won't find your pitch fork when you need it next is wherever you left it. "He moves that pitchfork every time someone puts it down," Katrina explained.

Sudden loud and unexplained crashes are also heard periodically and no reason for the racket is ever determined. Recently, a ranch-hand working alone in the shop distinctly heard someone come into the building and walk across the concrete floor. Not unusual perhaps, at a busy ranch, except that there was no one there—not that the hand could see, anyway.

That particular employee's wife has actually seen Ed Marsten. He came to her in what may have been a dream. The woman, a comparative new-comer to the establishment, was resting on a couch in the main ranch-house when she saw the image of a man. When she arose, she described the vision to her fellow ranch residents, who immediately recognized the description as that of the long-deceased Ed Marsten.

Ed hasn't restricted his ghostly presence to people who actually lived on the ranch, either—he's spooked the occasional guest at the place too. By now Ed Marsten's ghost has become an accepted entity on his former ranch.

LORI'S GHOST

At the end of a meeting in Edmonton, the lady I'd been interviewing recommended that I contact her sister in Calgary. "Her daughter-in-law has quite a story to tell," Mary Bruce advised.

A few months later, while listening to Lori's tale, I thought back to those words and realized what an understatement Mary's advice had been.

"Everyone just calls him my ghost because he's always followed me," Lori began.

Lori's haunting experiences began when she was a teenager. She and the rest of the members of her family were aware that there was something unusual going on, but no one addressed the feeling until one day Lori had a friend visiting. The young man sat chatting with her in the living-room, until something in the hall appeared to catch his eye. Completely distracted from their conversation, the visiting teen stared intently into the hall, as though watching something. Knowing that her friend was just seeing what all her family had been seeing, she attempted to reassure him.

"Oh, don't mind him. He's our ghost," Lori explained.

That was the first time anyone in the family had acknowledged to another person a phenomenon that they'd been living with for some time. The family member who was most aware of the strange presence was their mongrel dog, ironically named Spooky. The mutt didn't accept the ghost nearly as easily as the human members of the family did. Spooky became very agitated when he sensed the spirit and would pace back and forth growling. Once the animal was barking at an unseen force in the kitchen. Lori's mother picked the dog up and tried to carry it into the kitchen. "That was the only time Spooky ever bit anyone," Lori recalled.

Whatever was in the kitchen obviously had Spooky spooked. His owners shared the dog's concern when tin plates began to come off the kitchen wall, removed by some unseen force. Little did Lori suspect at the time that these occurrences would become so frequent that she would grow to almost count on them.

"I'm a very methodical person," Lori explained. For this reason, even as a teenager, she liked to keep her belongings in an orderly manner and know where everything was at all times. "But things started just disappearing and then reappearing," she added.

Around this time, Lori left home to live with a young couple. It didn't take the ghost long to track Lori down. When pictures hung in her new home began coming off the walls and a kitchen cupboard door cracked in half in the middle of the night, Lori knew that her ghost had found her.

During this period the girl returned home briefly to help her mother settle into new accommodations. While Lori was gone from the couple's home, they heard a baby crying there. They had children, but not a baby. They couldn't find the origin of the cries. Only Lori's return some days later put an end to the mysterious sounds.

Lori moved again, this time into an nearly new townhouse. "My cat was psycho the whole time I lived there," she remembered. "One day I went out and left the drapes open. When I came back, they were closed. I was terrified to go into the place but when I did, there was no one there."

If that prank wasn't enough to let Lori know that it had followed her once again, the persistent ghost went back to his old tricks of taking pictures off the walls. The young woman remembers the time living in the townhouse as a "bad experience."

Once again Lori moved, this time into the basement apartment of her future in-laws' home.

"I was home alone one New Year's Eve. I heard footsteps coming down the basement stairs, then doors opening and closing. But there was no one there. Another time someone got into bed with me. I had a water-bed and I could feel someone get into the other side of the bed," she recalled.

Petrified, Lori eventually corralled enough courage to roll over and face her unwelcome companion in the bed. There was nothing there. "But you could see an indentation…where someone's body had been," she added.

Lori always knew that her unseen and unwanted companion was around. "The footsteps were always there and pictures would never stay on the walls," she remarked. The young woman's patience grew thin.

Suffering from badly strained nerves as a result of being forced to share her life with this presence, Lori lost her temper and yelled at the spectre. "I told him off," she explained. This solution brought temporary peace, but when Lori's daughter was born, the ghost returned to visit the child.

"When [my child] told me about a man being in her bedroom, I'd really had enough. I told her never to talk to him again. Then I yelled at [the ghost] again and told him I was throwing him out and that I didn't ever want him to come back. Every night for three years I pictured a white light around our house. I knew that [that] light would protect us. He hasn't come back and it's been seven years now," she added.

Lori never actually saw her ghost. Despite not seeing it, she's sure that it was male. The being lacked a distinct size or form, although once when she felt his presence she did see a shadow that had no apparent source.

This young woman had no hesitancy in sharing her story for publication, except for a concern that it might attract her follower once again.

I asked Lori to let me know if he did come back, although, other than allowing me to feel guilty about helping to destroy Lori's newfound serenity, I'm not sure what my knowing would have accomplished. Thankfully she hasn't contacted me and so we can presume that Lori is still sharing her life only with living beings.

HAUNTED HOUSE
NEAR HOLDEN

"We have no idea who Carl S. was or why he's buried under our house." Greg stated flatly.

Maybe not, but with a such an extraordinary situation, it's not surprising that Greg and Allan's house near Holden, southeast of Edmonton, is haunted. The two men have done just enough research into the history of their place to satisfy themselves, without (possibly) disturbing anyone else's painful memories. "I suppose we could approach the family and ask," Greg acknowledged. "They're still in the area."

The men's total acceptance of their unusual housing situation may be surprising, but it is also at least as obvious as their great affection for their house. That acceptance wasn't always the case, however. Allan especially was slow to warm to the home. An incident that occurred shortly after they moved in could have convinced them both to seek an alternative investment.

"There are entrances to the basement from the inside and the outside," Greg explained. "One evening in the fall, shortly after we moved in, we were watching television. Our dog, an Irish setter named Red Dog, was asleep [near us]. All of a sudden, Allan and I both heard an incredible scream. It came from the basement. We both jumped up and rushed to the top of the stairs. Neither one of us wanted to go down there after hearing that scream but we did. There was nothing there. Nobody. We checked the door that leads directly from the outside to the basement and it was locked."

Once their heart rates settled back to normal, Greg and Allan realized that there had been something else odd about the experience. Their dog had slept through the ear-piercing shriek. That certainly wasn't typical behaviour for any dog.

"We both would have felt better about going down into that basement if Red Dog had been with us," Greg chuckled. "But it was as if he didn't even hear [the scream]."

The incident spurred Allan's curious nature. "[Allan] is a great one for exploring and not long after we heard the scream, he was rooting around outside the basement entrance," Greg acknowledged.

The man's investigations were initially rewarded by finding that the builder had inscribed his name and the date that he built the house on a piece of wood near the entrance to the basement. That, of course, didn't do anything to solve the mystery of the scream, but it did help to prepare them when, some time later, Allan discovered a second inscription on a floor joist in the basement. This one read, "Here lies Carl S. 1917."

Knowing that someone has been buried under your house for eighty years certainly suggests as many questions as it answers. For this reason, Allan and Greg decided that they wanted to learn a little more about their property.

"The original farmhouse was located sort of in our backyard," Greg recalled discovering. He reasoned that the family had buried their little boy in their yard, near their house. Then in 1940, when those original homesteaders decided to build a new house and chose the spot where they'd laid Carl to rest twenty-three years before, they no doubt felt compelled to honour the deceased by carving the tribute.

"We presume that to lessen the impact of what they were doing, they devoted the house as a monument [to Carl]," Greg added.

The odd combination of a burial and subsequent construction on the same spot, presumably by the same family, would help anyone understand why the house might be haunted. What, though, other than that isolated and apparently source-less scream from the basement, lead Allan and Greg to accept that Carl's spirit is in their house?

"We've become friends with the woman who sold us the house. We invited her to supper one day. While we were chatting at the table, we said to her, 'When we bought this place, we didn't know it was haunted.' She laughed but she wasn't surprised. The people she'd bought the house from had gone to a lot of time, effort and expense fixing the place up. They moved in but they moved back out again almost immediately. Apparently the man was never comfortable in the house. He didn't like being alone in it," Greg said.

The man's reaction was understandable to both Greg and Allan, not only because it so closely matched Allan's original attitude, but because both men had accepted that when you were alone in the house, you felt as though someone was with you.

Despite all the evidence of his existence, Carl has kept a remarkably low profile.

"One summer evening we were returning from the city. It was about 10 or 11 at night. We had Red Dog with us in the van, so he hadn't been in the house to guard it. When we pulled into the driveway, we could see into the bathroom. There was a light on. We knew that we'd turned all the lights off before we left. We walked up to the back door, expecting to confront an intruder. We only got as far as the kitchen before we realized there was no light on anywhere [in the house] and there was no one in the house. The front door was still locked and no one had gone out the back door," Greg remembered.

Discovering everything to be normal, however, did nothing to shake their belief in what they had seen from the van – there definitely had been a light on in the house when they drove up. The men merely mentally filed the incident with the isolated scream that they'd heard and the constant feeling of a presence in the house.

Allan and Greg, as owners of the house, aren't the only ones to feel that their home has something of a personality, perhaps as a result of the long-deceased Carl's spirit pervading the place.

"Many people who visit describe this house as a warm and friendly place. Whoever is here, and I truly do believe that someone is here..." Greg began, but let the thought trail off.

Enough had been said. The story of their haunted house had been told. No further explanation was possible or needed.

ONE GHOST PER BLOCK

There is no doubt that some locations are more haunted than others. A quick check into the history of an extremely haunted area will often explain the concentration of spirits. For instance, it isn't surprising that places of great trauma or tragedy such as the Frank Slide area in southwestern Alberta are veritable hotbeds of ethereal activity.

There is, however, a cluster of ghosts in an otherwise ordinary part of our provincial capital that is truly puzzling. The area in question runs along 103rd Avenue across 122nd Street, 123rd Street and on to 124th Street. Stranger still is that these stories, which have come to me over the years from unrelated sources, don't seem to be connected in anyway except geography.

The first story from the neighbourhood was told to me on John Hanlon's radio show, *Wildrose Country*. A woman called in with the following story.

From 1960 to 1966 she had lived with her family at 10346 123rd Street. The house has been gone for years now, demolished to make room for a parking lot, but the caller remembered vividly the strange events that took place during those years.

"The ghost wasn't a constant presence in the house," she began. "It only appeared three or four times a year."

The apparition was that of a young girl, about seven or eight years of age. "She only appeared when I was alone in the house. No one else ever saw her," the woman explained. "She was dressed in white and had long hair."

The child's image would run past her, she recalled. Although the woman was understandably startled by the sight, she explained that "it wasn't frightening at all. I got used to it."

Where this occasional young visitor from beyond might have come from is nearly as puzzling as where she might be now, given that the house that she sometimes haunted has been torn down.

Less than a block away, in a high-rise apartment building, there's another female ghost, but this one is an adult.

"We first noticed her in about 1984," Floyd Pester stated calmly. Floyd and his wife, Heather, began noticing that small objects around their apartment would be moved about while they were out. Brass ornaments that had always sat in a particular pattern would be rearranged or even lying on their side, rather than standing up, when the couple came home. The Pesters were only mildly puzzled by the phenomenon until larger objects began being moved. It was then that they discovered that more than just their suite was involved.

"One day we came home and found a pitcher and jug set that [normally] sits on top of a dresser had been moved, and the jug was [now] lying on its side. The dresser sits over the hot-water heating unit, so I thought the building manager had been in our apartment while we were out. I asked her and she said 'No,' she hadn't been and asked what made me think she had," Floyd remembered.

Apparently the manager had good reason to be curious, for the building's ghost had also played tricks on her. "She told me that when she was alone in her apartment and in the tub," Floyd recalled, "she could often hear doors opening and closing."

This was a spirit that wanted lots of attention. Floyd explained that the controls for their stereo system were in their den and that there were speakers in that room and in the living-room. One evening Heather and Floyd were entertaining guests and so the stereo's volume control had been set to provide pleasant background music to their conversation.

"Suddenly [the stereo's sound level] went from background to booming," Floyd said. He added that there was no one in the den near the stereo's controls at the time. Perhaps the entity merely wanted the Pesters' attention diverted from their guests and back to her.

Floyd's cousin, who lived in the same building, a few floors below the Pesters' suite, acknowledged that he also knew of the poltergeist's presence in his own apartment. "[My cousin] would come home and find his balcony door open or his screens adjusted," Floyd said.

When his cousin went away on a trip, he asked Floyd to water his plants for him.

"Just inside his door there was a storage room," Floyd recalled. "He had a deep-freezer in there. It was plugged into the light socket with an extension cord, so I didn't want to do anything with the light switch. All I did was open the freezer door and feel for the cold. When my cousin got home, he asked me if I'd been into his storage room. I told him that I had, and explained why. He told me I could have turned the light off [when I left the room]. I told him that I never turned it on."

After a few occurrences like this one, the two men nicknamed the entity Cob. "It's short for Cobra," Floyd explained. "Because she's sneaky."

He recalled a trick that the spirit played while the two men were together. "We were in my cousin's apartment, getting ready to go out. We were both in the hallway putting on our shoes and all of a sudden the taps in the kitchen turned on," Floyd said with a chuckle. He went on to add that water faucets aren't the only things in the haunted building that turn on when no one's near them. "Lights will turn on too."

Floyd explained that there had been a suicide at the building some years ago when a woman killed herself by jumping from her twelfth-floor suite. Is this the only reason that he thinks of the ghost as female? No, Floyd Pester has a much more concrete reason for believing that their resident spirit is a female: "I've seen her," he told me. "I was sitting in the den and I watched my wife walk past, then my cat and then my wife. There were three of them and the first one wasn't my wife because she [the one who was really my wife] followed the cat."

Floyd isn't the only person to have seen the apparition. "People say they see her walking along the hallway and around the corner. Then she's gone," he explained. "Even visitors can sense her, and our cat, Wilberforce, is very aware of her. He certainly reacts to something and we're way up on the eleventh floor. There's no traffic that could be bothering him."

With all this paranormal activity, are the Pester's ever uncomfortable in their haunted high-rise? Floyd Pester's reaction was completely matter-of-fact and probably revealed a very pragmatic nature.

"Oh, no. She's never done anything bad. She just likes to play little pranks," he quipped.

The tenants in a smaller apartment building only two blocks away were not able to accept their ghost quite as calmly. Janice Tuff, who lived in the building for a year and a half during the mid-1980s, was relieved to report that she had never actually seen anything ghostly. "When I first moved in, there was no one living in the apartment under mine and yet I heard footsteps. They were heavy, like work boots on a tile floor," she recalled. "The sound was strongest in my kitchen. I didn't think much about it at first, except that it was more walking than would be necessary in a place that size."

Once the lower suite was rented out, however, Janice realized that she might have reason for concern. "I had been out one evening and the next morning the tenant from downstairs knocked on my door to tell me that I'd been walking around like an elephant all the night before and would I please keep it down," Janice reported.

Some co-workers of Janice's had also lived in the building. They had by now begun to tell her some very strange stories of their own about the little apartment block. Having heard those stories, and knowing that her suite had been vacant the previous evening, Janice was on guard against alarming the new tenant. She merely apologized and assured the woman that she'd make a point to walk more quietly.

One man whom Janice worked with had actually lived in the suite that she now called home. He recalled thinking of his apartment as the safe suite.

"A friend of his also lived in the building at that time. Strange things would happen in her apartment. For instance, the stereo would come on in the middle of the night. She would seek refuge with him," Janice recalled.

While her suite had a reputation as being a good one, there was also a "bad" suite that seemed to have a very bad effect on anyone who tried to live there. There was a rumour that one tenant in that suite had been so affected by the ghostly carryings-on that she'd become a complete recluse. Tenant scuttlebutt had it that the presence had frightened her so much that not only did she become an urban hermit who never left her apartment, but that she had built a box in her apartment and that she lived inside it.

What could account for such a destructive presence in a seemingly ordinary apartment building? Often when a place is as haunted as that building seemed to be, it becomes difficult to tell what is cause and what is effect. In the 1920s, thirty years before the apartment block was built, there was a murder at that address. The ghost could conceivably be the spirit of the victim, justifiably angered at his life being snuffed out prematurely.

Of course it is impossible to know for sure who the spirit is. What can be documented with certainty, however, are the noisy apparently sourceless footsteps, the sightings of the apparition, the very ghost-like activities involving electrical equipment and the unfortunate series of events that have plagued the building.

"There were stains in the hallway and people said they were from gasoline when someone had tried to burn the place down," Janice said. That radical action could have been taken by someone under the spirit's influence, it could have been an attempt to destroy what someone may have felt was an evil place, or it could have been completely unconnected to the haunting.

Just seven blocks north of this ghostly concentration another entity existed for a time in the house that writer Mark Kozub and his roommates rented. Mark began his retelling of the events by explaining that all of the incidents took place within the first couple of months in which he lived in the house.

This situation isn't unusual and might indicate that an unpleasant spirit can be rendered impotent or even driven out completely by happy, positive, energetic occupants. Conversely, an empty house can become a virtual incubator for paranormal activity if a malevolent force is present.

Fortunately, the spirit that Mark and his friends temporarily shared their lives with was completely harmless and nonthreatening.

"My brother came to visit me one evening," Mark recalled. "I knew he was very tired. The next day he called me. He wanted to apologize for having acted strangely as he was leaving." Mark tried to reassure his brother by telling him that he hadn't noticed anything except his exhaustion. His brother's reply came as quite a shock to Mark.

"He said that as he was going out the door, he had glanced upstairs and was sure he had seen a little girl standing at the top of the stairs. That had really thrown him because, of course, he knew there was no little girl living in the house," Mark related.

Mark thought to mention his brother's concern to a young woman who was also living in the house. Her reaction surprised Mark. She told him that she'd frequently felt a draft right at the top of the stairs. "She said it wasn't the kind of draft you get from an open window, but more like the feeling you get when someone walks past you," he remembered.

Not long after the brother's visit, the crashes started. One night Mark was in bed when he heard a thunderous bang from the room directly above. "It was so loud that it sounded as though my filing cabinet might have fallen over," he described.

Mark checked it out immediately but found nothing out of place anywhere in the house. The crashing sound was not an isolated event. Other tenants heard the racket on other nights and Mark's roommate thinks that she too may have seen the ghost.

"One morning she asked me why I'd come into her room the night before when she'd been sleeping. I told her that I hadn't and she suggested I might have been sleepwalking," Mark related. He told the young woman that he doubted that possibility very strongly as he had absolutely no history of sleepwalking. "She was pretty insistent, though, that she'd wakened up through the night and that, just for an instant, she'd seen an image beside her bed. I don't know what it was she saw, I'm just sure it wasn't me," he attested.

Mark may have had one other experience with the spirit.

"It was in a dream," he began. "The kind you wake up from just terrified. In the dream I saw a little girl. She would have been about four years old. She told me that she was the spirit that haunted the house.

She said that she'd been murdered by her father and that he'd buried her out in the yard."

Mark had no way of knowing the effect that that particular anecdote would have on me. It was almost word for word a story that I'd heard from a completely different source.

Fellow ghost hunter Ron Hlady is the preservation technician at McKay Avenue School, Edmonton Public Schools' Museum and Archives. Ron is very attached to the stately old brick school, even though the place is not as haunted now as it once was.

Peter, the resident ghost who haunted the school for decades, has either left the building or is keeping a much lower profile these days than he once did. Ron was in the habit of communicating with Peter through a Ouija board. Lately, though, there's been no sign of the phantom, either through recognizable antics of his doing or through his responses to Ron on the board.

This absence of spirit at the school coincided with the publication of my earlier book. Of course we have no way of knowing whether Peter was annoyed with being written about and left McKay Avenue School for that reason, or whether his ghostly thirst for attention was satisfied by being the lead story in the book and he finally felt free to go on to his final reward. There is the possibility too that Peter's departure following the book's publication was merely coincidence.

Whatever the case, Ron no longer feels the presence of his old friend Peter the way he used to. He still, however, keeps a Ouija board at the school; as a matter of fact, he keeps two of them there. The first board Ron brought into the school was one he borrowed from his daughters' supply of toys. It may have originated as a toy but that Ouija board proved to be a powerful medium. Ron had so much success with the borrowed board that he decided to build his own from scratch. He reasoned that if he used his own time and talents to craft the transmitter/receiver, his connection with spirits would be enhanced.

Ron's theory failed him completely on one particular Saturday night. "Some friends of mine wanted to use the board with me. There were some things that [this woman] wanted to find out about her past," Ron explained.

He chose to use his homemade Ouija board but had no luck with it whatsoever. "It was cold," Ron said. "Then we tried the other board and we made contact right away. My friend found out what she wanted to know and then we took a break for a while."

When the trio went back to the board, they asked if there were any spirits out there who wanted to make contact with them. "The planchette went crazy," Ron reported. "It started doing figure eights all over the board. We decided to back off."

After another short break, the little group agreed to try it again.

"The second time we hung in there and we questioned it further. It was the spirit of a little girl about six years old. She said she'd been murdered by either her uncle or her father and that she was lost in a plain with no one to talk to," Ron recalled. "After we talked to her for a while, she settled right down."

It's not much of a stretch for anyone to confuse a four-year-old with a six-year-old. Could the image in the house along 110th Avenue be the same spirit that Ron and his friends inadvertently contacted? To me the similarities in the stories are too close to dismiss.

FAMILY HOME IS HAUNTED

Just before Rose Zalasky began high school, her parents decided to sell their first house and relocate to a larger one.

"I remember they took us to see two houses. The first one was a new house and I loved it. The second was an older place and I hated it. I felt uncomfortable in it," Rose remembered.

The girl expressed her preferences but unfortunately her parents bought the older home, a decision that may have been responsible for damaging the structure of the family.

The new place was only a few blocks from the high school Rose would be attending, so at least the location worked well for the girl. Sadly, that was about the only aspect of the house that she enjoyed at all.

"Every time I walked across one part of the basement floor, the hair on the back of my neck would stand up," she explained.

Rose became convinced that there was a malevolent presence in the house and that it was strongest in the basement. She told her parents, who thought she had an overactive teenage imagination.

"I've discovered since then [her time in the haunted house] that what I actually do have is a sixth sense," Rose continued. "Even then I knew I could definitely feel something. Besides, my dog would even act strangely. He would stand at the top of the stairs and bark and bark when there was no one in the basement. The cats would act weird too. Finally, I decided to ask the neighbour whether anything had ever happened in the house. At first he denied that anything had happened and then he said that he should talk to my parents about it but eventually I got him to admit that there had been a suicide in the house," Rose said.

At least now Rose had some verification for her feelings of discomfort. She had no idea at the time how much more there was to come.

"One day one of my brothers and I were alone in the house," she recounted. "Someone summoned us from the basement. We heard 'Dave, Rose, get down here.' We ran to the basement stairs and called down, 'Is anyone there?' and there was no answer. The dog was standing beside us, barking. His fur was standing up."

Terrified, the two youngsters pushed the portable dishwasher against the closed basement door and ran to get the neighbour.

"He came in armed with a mallet and he checked all around but there was no one there," Rose said.

Despite the empty basement, both Rose and her brother were sure of what they'd heard. "I can't say for sure it was a voice calling us, but we were definitely summoned in some way or another," she affirmed.

The brother and sister tried to put the frightening incident behind themselves, especially as there was a lot happening in their home life. "About this time my parents started to have problems," explained Rose. "My father now attributes a lot of that to the atmosphere in the house."

One afternoon Rose invited a girlfriend home to play pool. The pool table was in the very haunted basement and the spirit did not hide itself from either Rose or her friend.

"I watched a little light bobbing through the room. Then it turned the corner and went down the hallway into my brother's bedroom. My friend saw the same thing only she saw a larger light." Rose paused in her story before continuing. "Then I somehow lost a few minutes. I don't remember anything but my friend said I was scaring her because I was chasing her around."

Whatever was in her family's home wanted attention and tried many different ways to get that attention. By way of an example, Rose recounted how "one time all the pool balls started to move [on their own]."

Desperate for some guidance and comfort, Rose turned to a trusted teacher. She knew that this man had deep religious convictions. She explained all that was happening in their home. The man suggested that the presence in the house was a demon of sorts. He counselled her to wear a cross at all times and to confront the spirit by saying the Lord's Prayer as she went downstairs.

"After that, it pretty much left me alone," she said.

"Did the evil presence leave?" I asked.

"No," Rose replied. "It never left. I always felt a presence in that house."

As the family grew, so did the number of people who were aware of the being. In one incident, the woman who became Rose's sister-in-law was lying on the bed in a basement bedroom. She heard a knock at her door and, thinking it was Rose's mother, called out, "Come in." The door remained closed but the knock was repeated. "Come in," the woman repeated but again the door remained closed. Wondering what the older woman might have wanted, she went upstairs to inquire.

"She asked my mother why she hadn't come into her room a few minutes ago," Rose commented. "My mother told her that she hadn't been downstairs at all. She explained that she'd been sitting doing her cross-stitch the whole time."

Although the evil atmosphere was strongest in the basement, the spirit did attempt to enter Rose's mother's bedroom once. "Mom felt something watching her," Rose remarked, "but she had a cross over her room door and I think that protected her."

Rose lived in the house with the evil spirit for eight years and not a day went by that she wasn't sorry her parents had chosen the house they did.

"It still gives me goose bumps to talk about it," she admitted. "My oldest brother will just joke about it. My middle brother is very quiet and he won't say anything. My other brother was too young. He says he remembers a bit but that's all."

As is so often the case with a haunted house story, it is impossible to know which came first: Did the former occupant's suicide cause a dreadfully negative force to be left in the house, or was the force already present so that it became a contributing factor in the suicide? What is known is that living in the house had a devastating effect on everyone in Rose's family.

CHAPTER 2

RELATIVES RETURN

A GHOST OF
CHRISTMAS PAST

In the early 1980s, Craig (a pseudonym) invited his mother to visit him in his new apartment. "He was so proud of his new place," the young man's mother informed me. "As I walked into the apartment I noticed a pair of his boots in the hall, by the door. I reached down to touch them and a realization struck me from out of nowhere. I knew that we wouldn't have Craig much longer."

Obviously, this thought was extremely distressing to the woman but, being a practical sort, she put it out of her mind as best she could. After all, her son was perfectly healthy and in the prime of his life. There was no reason at all to suspect this unbidden thought was anything close to accurate.

Tragically, less than two weeks later, that seemingly random thought proved to have been a premonition: Craig was dead, the victim of a road accident.

Craig's little niece, Lori, was a toddler at the time. She'd been the apple of her uncle's eye but, of course, was far too young to realize the implications of the family's dreadful loss. One afternoon, less than a year after the accident, Lori was visiting with her grandmother, Craig's mother.

"She sat at the dining room table happily colouring," Craig's mother remembered. "She looked up from her picture and toward the door to the house. She said 'Hi, Uncle Craig,' and then went back to her crayons without another word."

With great justification, Craig's mother felt that her son, Lori's uncle, was keeping a watch over them both that day. Perhaps he'd visited many times but his presence was such that it required the innocence of childhood to recognize it.

On Christmas Day 1995, Craig visited at his mother's home again. This time making his presence known to his mother, who was alone at the time. "I'd gotten up early on Christmas morning to prepare the food for later in the day," she told me. This was to be the first Christmas since Craig's death on which she would be hosting the family celebration, she observed. "I was at the kitchen counter with my back to the door when suddenly I felt Craig's presence. I knew he was there. I turned around and he was standing by the door, as clear as could be. Then he was gone."

The brief sighting of her deceased son was an extra Christmas present for the woman, who reported image was not at all unsettling. Quite to the contrary, she cherished the thought that, for the first time in nearly fifteen years, she would have seen all three of her children on the same day.

PLACING THE MONUMENT

Paul Anctil of Lethbridge spent the better part of his life crafting monuments, lasting memorials to those who had died. His son, Al, who has carried on his father's trade, distinctly remembers an event that affected his father deeply.

"The incident occurred back in the days when churches looked after the graveyards. They always had a special section for children who had died before they were baptized," he explained. "This was the case at St Pat's Church until there was a fire in the church and the records were destroyed."

After the fire and the loss of the cemetery plot diagrams, no one had any way of knowing exactly where a specific grave was unless it had been marked with a headstone. Despite this uncertainty, people would still occasionally decide that it was time to erect a monument in memory of their deceased relative. In one such case, a woman approached Paul and asked him to make a small monument acknowledging her deceased child's short time on earth.

When Paul Anctil finished carving the grave marker, he showed it to the woman who'd commissioned it and offered to go with her to the cemetery and help her place the marker. "Dad took the lady to the cemetery," son Al recalled. "He asked her where she'd like it placed. You must understand that a marker for a child is very small and can easily be carried under one arm. The woman indicated a spot and my father dug the stone into the ground."

The two were alone in their task at the cemetery that day. Nevertheless, just as Paul finished laying the stone, both he and the woman with him clearly heard a child's voice say, "I'm over here, Mommy."

In shocked silence, the pair moved the marker about 4.5 metres, to where the voice had come from. As they turned to leave, the same small voice sighed, "Thank you."

VISION SAVED HIS LIFE

The media have been wonderfully supportive of my efforts to collect ghost stories. I've received some terrific leads from radio station listeners and newspaper readers. The standard procedure is for the staff at the station or the paper to pass on to me the name and phone number of the interested party. For this reason, it surprised me when a woman I'd never heard of called one evening. She'd been given my number by a local radio station. Initially I was taken aback, but not for long. Meeting Mary Bruce was not only a treat, but she had two ghost stories to tell me and then led me to two more.

Mary's parents were immigrants from Ukraine. They came to Canada with another family—Mary's mother's sister and her husband. The pairing worked extremely well. While Mary's father worked to establish a family farm in the Glenevis area, his brother-in-law found work in a mine. This way the families had a bit of an income before the farm produced sufficient crops to meet their needs.

One cold winter's day in 1935, Mary's uncle was away at the mine. Her father noted in the morning that the supply of firewood needed to be replenished. He decided to go into the woods to cut more timber and asked that his wife pack him a lunch.

He walked the 5 kilometres quickly and worked at felling and branching trees all morning. The sun shone brightly and the forest blocked the wind, so despite the low temperature, the man ate his lunch in comfort, enjoying his surroundings and perhaps reflecting on how well the difficult choice to emigrate had turned out. Content and temporarily warm in spite of the winter conditions, having a full morning's work and a satisfying lunch under his belt, the man began to doze off.

No sooner had he lost consciousness than he heard footsteps crunching through the snow. The sound jolted him awake and he looked up to see his brother-in-law, the miner, standing nearby. When he called out to the man, the image disappeared. Puzzled, Mary's father packed up his belongings and headed further into the forest to finish chopping wood.

When he arrived home that evening he was surprised to find the local store keeper waiting for him. As the store had the only phone for kilometres around, the proprietor frequently delivered messages to the surrounding farms. Today he had an especially sad communication for Mary's father. His brother-in-law, the one who'd awakened him from his midday nap, had died that afternoon in the coal mine more than 300 kilometres from where Mary's father saw him.

Significantly, if the apparition had not wakened him, Mary's father might also have died that day. On a day as cold as that, even in a spot that is temporarily warm, hypothermia can be a very real threat.

GRANDFATHER WATCHES OVER BOY

This story was passed along to me by fellow folklore collector Kathryn Carter.

A young family lived on an acreage just outside Edmonton in the 1970s. They had two small children and had just adopted a third, a Metis boy.

One evening Lana (a pseudonym), the children's mother, sat in a rocking chair beside the glass patio doors. She held her Metis child and watched as large flakes of snow fell on the deck beyond the patio doors. Her gaze through the window was aimless, her thoughts unfocused. Then, apparently out of nowhere, a Native man appeared, wearing only a loin cloth.

Lana's heart pounded as she watched the man pass through the glass doors without opening them. He appeared angry and hovered near her as she clutched the child protectively.

"What are you doing?" he demanded. Lana was too shocked to speak. The visitor continued, "I am this child's grandfather and guardian. I want to know what you are doing with him."

Stumbling through explanations, Lana tried to convey the love she felt for her chosen son. The Native man, seemingly placated, nodded and passed back through the doors and out into the night. Lana never forgot her unusual visitor.

Some months later, the baby became ill. Lana called a friend and asked that he babysit the other children while she and her husband took the ailing boy to the hospital. As they arrived back home from their emergency trip, they saw their friend standing at the window anticipating their return.

"He was here!" exclaimed the friend as soon as Lana and her husband entered the house. Lana correctly assumed she knew exactly who the man was referring to, but for confirmation she asked, "Who was here?"

"Your son's grandfather was here. He demanded to know about the boy's health."

These visits from the boy's grandfather/guardian continued every time the baby fell ill. When the child outgrew his illnesses, the visits ceased.

GRANDMA COMES BACK FOR A VISIT

Some people know very early that they are especially intuitive or sensitive. Although she was only a youngster, about twelve years old at the time, Rose remembers knowing exactly when her grandfather had died.

"I pinpointed the minute my grandpa died. I woke up at ten minutes to two in the morning and I called out, 'Mom, he's dead!' My mother told me to go back to sleep. Twenty minutes later the phone rang. My grandfather had died."

Before she hung up, Rose's mother asked when the man had died. The answer was 1:50 am, exactly the time Rose had wakened and shouted the tragic news.

Rose's experiences of this kind didn't end with childhood—read this next anecdote:

"When I was an adult, married with two kids, I was driving along in the car one day and I suddenly felt my grandmother's presence. I even smelled her perfume. It smelled like lilacs. For just a second I got goose bumps but then I just got a warm feeling. My grandmother was a really good person," she explained.

Her visit with Rose was not the deceased woman's first. "When my grandmother died she visited my mom. She told her 'everything's all right.'"

Both women felt reassured after being made aware that the older woman they both still loved and missed had, in fact, remained a presence in their lives.

KING'S GHOST

This tale is positively ancient by Edmonton standards. It was told by local historian Tony Cashman on Halloween in 1953 and is also included in his book of Edmonton stories. The story appears here with Mr Cashman's kind permission. He tells the gruesome tale this way.

The events we're about to relate occurred in Fort Augustus, on Edmonton's Rossdale Flat, in January of 1803. They're noted in the diary of that hard-headed Scotch trader, John McDonald of Garth. McDonald was at that time director of North West Company operations on the Upper Saskatchewan. The story concerns a company trader named King; McDonald does not record King's Christian name, nor anything about him. In the diary of a rival company official, however, King is described as a bully.

In that January, word came in from a Native camp that they would like to trade. King was detailed to go out and trade on behalf of the North West Company, and it was learned through the grapevine that a hot-tempered trader named La Mothe would be there to bargain for the rival XY Company. The Native camp was a day's journey away and King planned to be gone three days. On the eve of his departure, as King fitted up his sleighs, the master of the Hudson's Bay Company's Fort Edmonton came over to talk. He said: "Take care, King. Be careful of La Mothe. La Mothe may shoot you." King, boisterous and loud, laughed off the warning. "To be shot by La Mothe... That would be a good joke indeed."

Next morning he set out for the Native camp, in high spirits and in high glee over the fears of the Hudson's Bay Co. man. Two nights later, King's wife, a Native woman, was sleeping in their tent at Fort Augustus, with their six-year-old daughter sleeping beside her. There was a strong fire burning to keep out the January cold. In McDonald's diary he calls it a "clear, rousing fire." Suddenly Mrs King was wakened by a plaintive whimper from the little girl. The little girl said uneasily, "Mother, there is father at the foot of the bed...his neck is all red."

Mrs King quieted the six-year-old, assured her that it was just a dream, and if she would just go back to sleep everything would be all right. Later in the night, when the fire had burned lower, the little girl was sitting up in bed again. "Mother," she whimpered, "there's father at the foot of the bed. His neck is red."

Once again the mother coaxed her daughter off to sleep. The next morning she told the strange story to many people in the fort, including the man who has passed it down to us, John McDonald of Garth. But as McDonald himself wrote: "Nothing was thought of it..." until afternoon.

They saw King's party returning to the Fort; but there was no sign of King until the sleighs pulled in. Then they saw him lying in the bottom of the sleigh. He was dead, shot through the throat. He had been shot by La Mothe in a violent argument. La Mothe was arrested and sent to Montreal for trial. There he pleaded self-defense in the shooting and was acquitted. King was buried on Edmonton's Rossdale Flat with the full military honours of the North West Company.

And that's the end of the story. The case was sealed and closed except for one thing. Did the spirit of King actually return to Rossdale that night nearly two hundred years ago? Did he really pause for a last look at his sleeping child before passing into the eternal beyond? If he did, he was a gentle spirit, a ghost no one need fear.

UNKNOWN SISTER
PROVIDES PROTECTION

For years, David Gell hosted extremely popular weekend morning shows on CBC Radio. He frequently invited me to do interviews with him, which he later broadcast. It was gratifying to see how often these conversations would bring responses from the public. The following is one such story. In order not to lose any of the flavour of the tale it is reprinted as George Wood wrote it in his letter to me.

My father was a railroader—not given to contemplating "the number of angels that could dance on the head of a pin," a practical man, matter-of-fact—a man as sane as a hammer!

He left school at fourteen, having lost a year in bed to rheumatic fever. He went immediately to work. Life was tough. Making a living was not easy and left little time for philosophizing.

Here, then is a story he told me when I was sixteen or seventeen and finishing high school. It amazed me, for I had never seen this dimension of the man.

He worked for the old Grand Trunk Western Railroad (GTW). After five years on the job he received his first pass. This entitled him to free passage anywhere in western Canada where the GTW had track.

When his holiday time rolled around he decided to travel from his home in Portage la Prairie to Edmonton where his mother's sister lived with her family. He had no intention of staying with them but promised his mother he would "look in." When he made his visit Aunt Lou would hear of no other arrangement than that he stay with them.

The family regarded Aunt Louise as somewhat "strange" as she was known to have more than a passing interest in spiritualism and the occult. He slept there and took his meals with the family but beyond that chose to make himself scarce; busy with what any young man of nineteen or twenty might do—seeing the sights of the "big city." What sights and how big the city might be judged by knowing that this would have been about 1912 or 1913.

At the evening meal a day or two before he was to leave Aunt Lou announced that she was to have a seance the next evening. Although she'd never met the person it delighted her to report that "one of the country's leading mediums" was to preside. She had been disturbed to learn that one of the eight guests invited to participate would be unable to attend.

"Jack, I wonder, would you care to sit in?" she asked.

He was caught, lost for any kind of a plausible excuse.

As the group sat down to the table the medium announced that he sensed the presence of an "unbeliever." Dad in his turn "sensed" whom he meant. He regarded the entire event as a fraud.

The medium then turned to him.

"Jack, do you know a little girl named Mary?"

"No," Jack replied.

"That's strange. She's standing behind your chair and says she has a message for you. She says she wants you to know that she is your guardian angel and that you are not to worry about accidents at work. She will protect you from all harm."

The medium then went on to describe her appearance. She was blue-eyed, her hair, which was dark she wore combed straight back and it fell to her waist. In it was a ribbon holding it in place and matching her dress which was [made of] white material with purple violets and hung to mid-calf. She wore white stockings and black patent leather shoes. Her age, the psychic judged, to be "about eight years."

My father remained skeptical and did his best to put the whole evening out of his mind. Nothing he had heard made any sense at all.

He arrived back at home [in Portage la Prairie] near supper hour and as the family gathered about the table everyone wanted to know about his holiday, about Aunt Lou and her family. He, quite naturally, related the story of the seance.

When recreating the scene for me Dad said that his parents were visibly shaken, so much so that they could not continue their meal. Later that evening having regained her composure my grandmother revealed the reason for their agitation. Mary was their first-born child.

She had died of diphtheria before their second child was a year old. They had decided not to tell the other children until they were "of an age" and later "not to tell them at all." The apparel, as described, was exactly that in which Mary had been buried, accurate to the most minute detail.

How could anyone have known? Aunt Lou knew of the death, of course, but had not attended the funeral and would not therefore have known of the clothing. Grandmother had not revealed those details in any of the infrequent correspondence that passed between the two families. It would be highly unlikely as well that Aunt Lou would have shared any such personal family information with a man she was meeting for the first time.

Mary had been eight at the time of her death.

My father told me this story but never mentioned it to my older brother or sisters. That, he left to me. They were incredulous. Why had he chosen me? Did he perceive in me a more accepting sensibility? Had he come over the years to accept his "guardian angel?" I am left with these questions.

Retiring after nearly fifty years of railroading and despite many close calls, some in which others were gravely injured, he never had an accident. His sister Mary did her job well.

A VISIT FROM
UNCLE MARSHALL

Al Anctil of Lethbridge is a middle-aged man by now, but he clearly remembers an unusual visit from a relative during his childhood.

"I was just a little fellow at the time. I was sleeping with my brother who was nine years older than me. I woke up and turned over. There was a man sitting [on a chair] beside our bed," he recalled. "I was terrified and pulled the covers over my head."

The frightened child's attempts to hide under the covers woke his brother.

"Are you sick or something?" the older boy inquired of his obviously distressed sibling.

"No," Al remembers replying. "But I saw a man sitting beside the bed."

"Who was it?" his brother asked.

"I don't know. I've never seen him before," Al replied.

In characteristic older-brother fashion the boy told Al in no uncertain terms that he had seen no such thing and should go back to sleep.

"The next morning when we got up, the chair where I'd seen the man sitting and watching us was still pulled up beside our bed. Of course my brother said I'd put it there, but I hadn't," Al explained.

The incident was largely forgotten until one day when the children were looking through some old family photographs.

"That's him," Al remembers announcing excitedly after examining a particular snapshot. "That's the man who was sitting beside our bed that night."

The person he identified was his Uncle Marshall, who had died even before Al's older brother had been born. Perhaps the deceased man merely wanted to enjoy a few minutes with the nephews he hadn't ever met.

A LOVE STORY

People who report encounters with spirits almost always indicate that the experience was an intense one. This story is certainly no exception, but in addition it is also a deeply intimate account involving three generations of the same family. For this reason, and because the family is so well known in the Lethbridge area, their identity has been disguised through the use of pseudonyms.

Ellie began the tale by acknowledging that she had never actually met her father-in-law, as he had died before she met her husband. Ellie was, however, extremely close to her mother-in-law, Nanny. The older woman had been widowed in very early middle age but remained very much in love with her husband. Nanny stayed on in the couple's home after her husband's death. Ellie spent a lot of time there, offering companionship and helping where she could.

"I always felt there was a presence in that house. I always felt there was someone looking out for me when I was there. My husband, Ron, said he too could feel something, but he wondered if the presence was his grandfather rather than his father," Ellie explained.

The question of the ghost's identity was answered when Ellie invited a friend to visit her mother-in-law's house. "My friend is a psychic and as we were going for lunch [near Nanny's house] I suggested we pop in," the woman told me. "My husband's grandfather had lived in that house too. He had lived a long time but my father-in-law was only in his forties when he died. My friend told me the presence in the house was the spirit of a younger man. She told me he was earthbound, waiting for someone."

From then on there was little question and no concern about who was haunting the old family home. "I always felt he was showing gratitude to me," Ellie said. "He was very kind to me. If I was tired I could lie down on a bed in that house and feel looked after."

Ellie wasn't surprised to learn that her father-in-law had been something of an amateur magician and a practical joker in his day. She'd long felt those personality characteristics were part of the atmosphere in her mother-in-law's house.

Neither Ellie nor her husband was concerned in the least about Nanny staying in an obviously haunted house. "We agreed this was not a foreboding presence," Ellie confirmed.

Nanny's good health held for years and years but eventually, even with help from Ellie and the rest of the family, the day came when she moved from her much loved home to a seniors' lodge. Selling the old place appeared to be an inevitability.

Ellie's sons, who were adults by then, were especially disturbed by that possibility. One of the young men, Murray, had just married. He and his bride, Katy decided they should buy the old place themselves. "It felt like it was a good decision," Ellie revealed.

Young Katy, however, was not so sure at first. "I always felt as though someone was watching me," she explained, the discomfort she'd experienced obviously still fresh in her mind. "My husband works nights.

I'd be in bed in the room that was his grandmother's and I could hear the squeaks of someone walking along the hall. The cats would stare and the hair on the backs of their necks would stand up."

One night as Katy lay in bed listening to the sounds of footsteps along the hallway making their way toward her bedroom door, she watched as the doorknob turned. "I got the impression that I shouldn't have closed the bedroom door," she told me. "I felt a presence come sweeping over me —checking me out."

On another day, the young woman fell asleep on the living room couch. "I woke up to the feeling that something was pulling me up from my body," Katy declared.

Katy's sister was also made to feel uncomfortable by the presence in the house. "My sister is very sensitive. One day she was visiting and then all of a sudden she left, saying, 'I've got to get out of here.'"

"I always felt there was something in the hall and I always got the impression I was being checked," Katy continued. "One morning, about 5, I was in the bathroom getting ready to go to work and I could hear music. It was a really old kind of music and at the same time I smelled something, something musty and sweet."

All of this evidence went even further to convince both Katy and Ellie that the spirit in the old house was that of Nanny's long-deceased husband. He had first lived with his wife and then watched over her in that house for so many years that they surmised he must have wondered who Katy was and why she was there where he thought his wife should have been. "Eventually, I think the ghost and I just got used to each other," Katy assessed.

Ellie added, "Nanny died in March 1995, and there hasn't been any activity since then. That man waited for her all those years."

Katy nodded in agreement. The presence that haunted the old Lethbridge house for nearly fifty years has finally been reunited with the love of his life. Together again at last, they have moved on to their final reward.

CHAPTER 3

GHOSTS IN PUBLIC

HAUNTED IN STONY PLAIN

In all my years of collecting ghost stories, my requests have rarely been as warmly received as they were at the Stony Plain Multicultural Centre. "We will be delighted to be included in your book," were the opening words of Margit Knupp, the curator at the centre.

What good news that was for me. Not only are the Multicultural Centre and the Oppertshauser House (next door) fascinating old buildings, they are also very haunted.

The Multicultural Centre was formerly the first high school in the County of Parkland. When it was constructed in 1925, the two-storey brick building sat in isolation, surrounded only by fields. By the time the Heritage Agricultural Society took over the building, it had been abandoned and left to deteriorate. The lovely old building had also become home to an assortment of spirits.

One of the main floor rooms in the centre has been decorated to represent a settler's cabin. Period artifacts have been so cleverly collected and assembled that by now both staff and patrons refer to the room simply as "the cabin." Visitors to the museum frequently report seeing "some old lady" in the cabin when the staff is fully aware that there is no one of this description in the room.

Ellen Green, an employee at the centre, remembers an instance when a local artisan was running an evening class in a part of the cabin done up to resemble a homesteader's kitchen.

"The instructor for the class had forty or fifty pounds of equipment with her. It had taken her three trips to bring it all into the building from her car. After the class was over and her students had left, the woman was packing up, getting ready to leave. She noticed that the temperature in the room was dropping and dropping until it became icy cold," Ellen recounted.

"The woman had keys to the place and was supposed to lock up and turn on the security system. Apparently, while she was putting her things away she suddenly felt someone staring at the back of her neck. The stare and the sudden extreme cold she was managing to tolerate but when she also felt some unseen presence demand that she leave the building, it became more than she could bear. The instructor was so unnerved by the feeling that she picked up everything she'd brought in and ran from the building. She got the building locked but she didn't take the time to set up the security alarm."

The next morning the woman phoned the centre. She was obviously still greatly troubled by her experience the evening before.

Ellen remembers being told that the woman was nearly unintelligible. "The [staff member] she was talking to thought at first that something unfortunate must have happened to her in the parking lot. She said she'd never ever come back."

After a time the woman calmed down enough to explain that she was sure there had been a ghost in the building and that whoever or whatever it was no longer wanted her there.

"It scared the living daylights out of her," Ellen recalled.

Ellen has never had a personal ghost experience in the centre but she is certainly well aware of the presence next door in the Oppertshauser House.

"One day, several years ago, in the summer, I was doing some typing in my office. It's on the upper level of the Oppertshauser House in a former bedroom. A woman about forty years old came up and started to talk to me. She told me that her mother had once worked cleaning in the house and that occasionally, as a youngster, she would go to work with her mother."

When the visitor left, Ellen went back to her typing. "Immediately after she left, I noticed a smell. It was a men's cologne, one that I didn't recognize. I didn't think too much of it until I realized that we didn't have any men on staff at the time except a maintenance man who worked at night. I got up from my desk to investigate. The smell was everywhere and nowhere. I brought other people up to my office and they smelled it too."

The sweet smell continued intermittently over the next two weeks and gradually faded. No source for the odour was ever found. Ellen is convinced that there is a connection between the woman's visit and the sudden arrival of the fragrance.

"I think the woman's visit caused some sort of disturbance in the force," she surmised.

The wafting odour wasn't the only evidence of disturbance. "We have ice-cream–parlour type chairs in one room upstairs. We would leave them around a table in the centre of the room but we'd always come back to find them up against the wall." Ellen explained.

One of her co-workers thought Ellen had been moving them and the woman spoke to her about it.

"Have you got a problem with those chairs?" she asked Ellen. When they informed one another that they certainly weren't the ones responsible for the furniture rearrangement, the women realized that this too had begun occurring just after the visit by the woman who was once connected with the house and its original owners.

Like the cologne odour, the strange movements also stopped occurring over the next two weeks, and neither has ever returned. Neither has the woman who, as a youngster, used to visit the house frequently.

Another employee, Debbie Truckey, actually saw a man's face as she was locking up the Multicultural Centre.

"It's a very short story," she explained with a nervous laugh. "I saw the face and I ran."

Thankfully, after some gentle prodding, Debbie related the incident in more detail.

"I was alone. I had the late shift on a Sunday night. Fortunately it was summer, so it wasn't dark. I was locking up and when I got to the south doors by the Oppertshauser House, I looked up and saw a face," she recalled.

Although she didn't recognize the man's face from any pictures she'd ever seen in the centre, she did notice that "his collar was funny—it was high and white."

Startled, Debbie fled from the building. She is happy to report that she never saw the face again.

Both the Oppertshauser House, now an art gallery, and the centre—with its museum, archives, gift shop and tea house—are open to the public.

THE FORT SASKATCHEWAN JAIL

"The Fort." To anyone on either side of the law, anywhere in western Canada, those two words meant only one thing—the jail at Fort Saskatchewan. The provincial government began building this foreboding-looking institution in 1913. Right from the beginning, its history was as unpleasant as it was colourful.

Less than two years after the first sod was turned to begin construction, the jail hosted its first hanging. On October 6, 1915, thirty-year-old George Leek was hanged from the neck until he was dead—the first in a long list of executions in the old jail.

On November 22, 1922, Florence Lassandro, the only woman ever to be hanged in Alberta, kept her gallows date with Arthur Ellis at the Fort Saskatchewan Jail. This, despite the fact she was likely innocent of any indictable offence, guilty only of naiveté.

Twenty-two-year-old Robert Cook, convicted of the gruesome murders of his father, his step-mother and five half-brothers and sisters, holds the distinction of being the last person ever hanged in Alberta. He dropped to his death at the end of a rope on June 26, 1959, while continuing to protest his innocence.

Although the jail remained in use for many years after that, capital punishment had been outlawed and so the gallows area of the jail was the one of the first to be abandoned. Of course, not everyone who died at the jail was executed. Over the years several prisoners died from natural causes while serving time. Often these men had lost touch with any family they may have had and no one claimed their bodies. To offer the deceased some of the dignity in death that they missed in life, a section of the prison grounds was turned into a graveyard and inmates assigned to the metal shop made simple crosses as grave markers. Today the jail has been demolished but the cemetery remains. The area around the impersonal graves is virtually alive with the spirits of those wasted lives. Their presence can be felt by even the least sensitive visitor.

Fort Saskatchewan Jail

Before its demolition, the old jail stood empty for five years, while controversy raged around it. One side of the argument held that the cavernous place should be destroyed to make room for more commercially viable buildings. A second, equally motivated and vocal group, wanted the prison preserved in some form or another. This latter congregation held a number of disparate ideas about what form the old jail's future should take. While this lack of agreement made for stimulating discussions, it also served to splinter the preservationists' campaign and so, on August 16, 1994, the wreckers moved in. Within a week the eerily empty old place had been reduced to a pile of rubble.

Shirley MacLeod, an energetic young wife and mother living in Fort Saskatchewan at the time of the controversy, stood staunchly in the preserve-the-jail camp. She believed that the old place could continue to serve the community—and even all of Canada—if it were turned into a museum reflecting the country's history of law enforcement. She and others worked long and hard—and, as it turned out, unsuccessfully—to protect the jail from destruction. Less than a year before it was torn down, Shirley, her husband, Kent, and their daughter Elizabeth joined a half-dozen other interested people on a tour of the deserted penitentiary.

A former guard, Al, offered to serve as a guide during the excursion. The tour was a thorough one, including even areas that the public would not normally want to see.

"We walked through the kitchen and then on to the room where the prisoners about to be hanged were kept," Shirley recalled. "He showed us the room where death-row inmates were kept. It had one small window that only allowed a prisoner to see outside where the gallows were being built for him. On our way, Al pointed out the stairway leading to the gallows outside. A space beside that gallows staircase was partially lit from lights we had turned on along our way. An ordinary kitchen chair sat in the corner. Liz and I noticed a person huddled on the floor in the corner behind the chair."

Then, just as quickly as it had appeared, the image disappeared.

Swinging around to her daughter, Shirley exclaimed, "Did you see that?"

The youngster was so unnerved by the sight that she could only respond with a monosyllabic "Yeah."

"I asked her what she saw to make sure we were talking about the same thing. She said, 'There was a guy in the corner but he disappeared.'"

Shirley reported the sighting to the guard/tour leader, who wasn't surprised at all and added that whenever he walked through the place he got an eerie feeling and fully expected to be confronted by a ghost.

Because the jail itself is no longer there, none of us will ever know whether or not we might have had a chance to see the ghost of the frightened man for ourselves, but a trip to the Fort Saskatchewan Jail cemetery should trigger even the most skeptical cynic's goosebump reflex.

As you approach the tiny, fenced-in graveyard, the first thing you will notice is the silence. If you've been chatting with a companion while walking toward the cemetery, your conversation will doubtless wind down as you come within sight of the anonymous plots. If there is any sound at all, it will only be the murmuring of the breeze in the prairie grasses, which somehow adds to the totality of the silence.

While you may be suspicious that your sense of hearing is not functioning at all, another sense, one we're not nearly as familiar with, will be working overtime. The hairs on the back of your neck will stand up and you will experience a couple of involuntary shivers or shudders that will leave your arms decorated with goose-bumps. It's a strange sensation and it's stranger still that this reaction is so predictable in that particular spot. Perhaps this is the feeling that one human soul gets when it becomes aware another human soul.

Perhaps this is the essence of a ghost story.

GHOSTS IN CALGARY'S OLD CITY HALL

Given our system of democratic rule, it is a given that anywhere legislation is enacted will become an arena for controversy. Controversy began swirling around Calgary's old City Hall even before the sod was turned for its construction, and controversy continues today, years after the building has been replaced by an impressive new facility. The debate before and during construction of the stately old sandstone structure centred around what were viewed as unnecessary delays in completing the building (it was under construction for four years) and a horrendous increase in the expenses involved (the final cost was twice what had been estimated).

Today the controversy is centred around the grand old building's ghosts. Are they really there? How many are there? Who were they and why do their spirits remain?

Information Officer Don Morberg has heard rumours that two ghosts have been seen in the building: one a man, the other a woman.

"The man may be a former prisoner who died years ago in the police lockup," he reports.

The identity of the female apparition is a little more difficult to pin down.

"She's seen on the old stairs," Morberg recounts. "We have no record of any female dying in the building. I've heard that she might be a former alderman's wife or perhaps a madam who had been locked up in the basement cells at one time."

Most of the sightings have been by the building's security personnel and, unfortunately, they aren't talking.

"They know something, that's for sure," attests a contract employee who asked not to be named but then went on to tell the story of a woman who fled an office, packing an enormous amount of heavy gear with her. The woman had been trying to do her job while ignoring the sensation of not being alone in a room where she presumed she was alone. Finally the uncomfortable feeling overpowered her work ethic and she left, announcing, "I'm not working in there tonight!"

At this writing the old City Hall, ghosts and all, is temporarily out of service. The building closed late in 1995 in order to undergo restoration and reconstruction. Hauntings are often disturbed during renovations, so the building's reopening in the spring of 1997 will be an interesting time, both for Calgarians and for ghost hunters everywhere.

CANMORE'S APPARITION

Despite my having better-than-average connections in the town of Canmore, this story eluded me for years. No one, it seemed, was comfortable talking about their experiences, even to trusted workmates—who would then have relayed the story to me. I'd pretty well given up any hope of ever hearing the whole story, when a fellow folklore buff sent me a copy of a write-up in an archival copy of the *Calgary Herald*. The thought-provoking story it contained was certainly worth the wait.

The events take place at the Canmore Community Centre, a complex that houses the town's arena and dance hall. Rink attendant Kevin Stevenson told the paper, "I don't know what it was. I don't know if it was a ghost and I really don't want to find out."

Kevin first saw the apparition in November of 1983. For fear of being teased, he kept the experience to himself, until he heard his coworkers discussing similar experiences.

"I was on the tractor driving around doing my last flood. I got this real spine-tingling chill. It felt like something was staring at you. I looked all over and didn't see anything. I looked up in the windows and saw this silhouette," Kevin said. "My eyes just started pouring water I was just so scared."

Kevin described the apparition as being small, with long hair. He mentally dubbed the image "little hippy."

Some years later, as he worked in the ice plant, Kevin heard footsteps on the boardwalk outside the door. He looked all around the Community Centre but the area appeared to be deserted and so he returned to his duties. The sounds of the footsteps, however, continued.

Tom Bisson confirmed some of Kevin's information. He had looked up at the window where the other man had seen the unidentifiable image. Tom described seeing a "wisp of a figure" staring at him.

Tom and Kevin even shared a couple of eerie experiences in the arena. One night they were working together when they distinctly heard a child call for its mother. Despite a thorough search of the complex they both knew well, they turned up nothing. They have also heard the unnerving sound of a dog growling, although there was no animal anywhere on the premises.

Tom summed up his feelings about the experiences this way: "We were all kind of leery to talk about it at first because we thought people would think we were crazy. But when it happens so often and so many have seen it, you just can't deny it."

Employees of a construction firm hired to do some work at the arena reported seeing what they presumed was a ghost and others have heard unexplainable noises coming from the second floor. Apparently you don't have to be working at the Community Centre to see the apparition. The girlfriend of the maintenance staff supervisor was not at all surprised to hear the stories told by the staff. She'd seen the ghost too but, like the others were at first, she was hesitant to speak of her encounter.

Speculation has it that a little girl drowned in the swamp that once existed where the complex is now located. It is said that her body was never recovered and many feel certain that hers is the spirit haunting the Canmore Community Centre.

They might be right.

HAUNTED BANKS

Many people dread going to work each day, but a few dedicated souls are so attached to their jobs that they continue to report for work even long after they have died! It's a fair bet that the two following stories are examples of this phenomenon.

Everyone in St. Albert knows that, despite the local Bank of Montreal Building's name, no one processes financial transactions there. Nevertheless, the stately seventy-five-year-old Georgian-style building is still always referred to that way even though it hasn't housed the Bank of Montreal, or any other bank, since 1989. It didn't even begin life as a Bank of Montreal.

The building's past is intriguing. Centrally located in downtown St. Albert, it was constructed in 1921 as the Banque d'Hochelaga. The contractor must either have been a budget-conscious person or a forerunner of today's recyclers, because he used bricks reclaimed from the failed Royal Hotel. This created the interesting circumstance of the building materials being considerably older than the actual building. It could also be a contributing factor to its status today as a haunted building.

The Banque d'Hochelaga did not survive the Depression and it closed its doors for good in 1936. Soon after, the building was reborn as a coffee shop—the Rainbow Inn. In its next incarnation it housed municipal offices. In 1955, however, the Bank of Montreal bought the building and it became a place of finance once again.

In 1989 the Bank of Montreal branch moved on to more up-to-date surroundings and the building that had been a landmark in the town for so long was declared a historic site. It sat empty for a while before local businesses began to see the appeal of situating themselves in this centrally located and historically significant building.

John and Denise Kilduff, owners of Clayworks, were tenants there for several years. There's little question in either of their minds that the old place is haunted.

"We have both heard footsteps from up on the second floor," John explained.

The noises came as something of a surprise to the couple.

"We'd didn't hear anything the first year but once the [upstairs tenant] moved out it got quieter. On several occasions when the second floor was empty we heard noises coming from there."

Because it sounded as though someone were walking around up there, the Kilduffs would investigate the sounds. But they always found the same thing: an empty second storey or, as John put it, "There was no human form."

The upstairs would originally have been used as the bank manager's living quarters. Perhaps one of the former employees has stayed on to enjoy his former home into eternity.

The Kilduffs have since moved their business but judging from the matter-of-fact way they speak of the time they spent in the haunted building, the phantom footsteps overhead weren't a factor in their decision to relocate.

The Kilduff's ghost story bears a remarkable resemblance to one told to me in Lethbridge. Elisha Rasmussen hosts a daily television show on CFCN in this southern Alberta city. The fact that it has been running for more than twenty years attests to Elisha's skills as a hostess and the show's popularity. Knowing of my renewed search for ghost stories, this warm and personable lady invited me to once again be a guest on her program.

"We'll open the phone lines. People can call and tell you your ghost stories," she offered enthusiastically. "It'll be great fun."

Sadly, our best-laid plans went badly awry, leaving CFCN's camera and audio crews wondering if their station was haunted. The phone lines, which had been tested and found to be working well the night before, simply refused to co-operate once we were on the air. Only one call made its way through to us.

The caller was the wife of a bank manager. In the course of her husband's career, the pair had moved all over our province. In one town they lived in an apartment above the bank.

"In the morning we would hear the sounds of metal coat hangers banging together as if someone was going through our bedroom closet," she told us.

At first this noise made the caller and her husband very uncomfortable. After all, jangling coat hangers make a pretty distinctive sound, not one you could easily write off as building noises. The woman and her husband were nowhere near the closet when they heard the sounds and they were certainly the only people in their bedroom.

"We got used to it, though," she added. "I always thought it was just some poor dead bank manager looking for something to wear again this morning."

If today's banks are looking for long-term relationships with their managers, they might do well to read the personnel manuals from years ago. After all, at least a couple of managers from that earlier time seem to have positively defined the phrase "loyal employee."

ALBERTA'S LEGISLATURE BUILDING

One of the few disappointments I suffered while researching and writing my earlier book on ghosts was not being able to confirm the oft-told story of the resident ghost in our stately old Legislature Building. I'd heard from numerous people that the halls of "the Ledge" were heavily haunted and I even found a paragraph about the ghost in Frank Dolphin's book, *The Alberta Legislature, A Celebration*. In spite of chasing these hints, innuendoes and leads all over town through every source I could find, I was eventually forced to admit defeat.

The story that I'd hoped would be one of the most intriguing in the book had apparently proven itself to be a non-story. Either my research was inadequate or I'd been given misinformed leads. In the end I accepted the word of the man who should know, Oscar Lacombe, then Alberta's Sergeant-at-Arms. Over coffee one pleasant spring afternoon Mr Lacombe patiently explained that he was behind all the ghostly rumours I'd heard about the Ledge. And he felt a strong personal obligation to clear the matter up for me as he firmly believed he had, inadvertently, started the rumour in the first place.

It seemed that when a newly hired security guard was about to work his first night shift in the stately government building, Lacombe decided to have a little fun at the rookie's expense. As he bid the man good night he added that he hoped the guard wouldn't have a problem with the ghost. Oscar Lacombe believed that that simple line, meant only as a tweak of teasing, was responsible for the long-standing story about there being a ghost in Alberta's political headquarters.

With that explanation the story became, to me, the big one that got away. And that's the way I left the haunted Ledge story until the fall of 1995, when I was doing an author-visit at a bookstore in a north-Edmonton shopping mall. These promotional stints are fun because often, even if people aren't interested in buying books, they will stop and say hello. That's exactly how I received the story behind the rumours of the ghost at the Ledge.

Sales had been gratifyingly steady during the afternoon by the time a man I judged to be in his mid-thirties approached me. From his closely cropped hair, I assumed that he was either a member of the armed forces or a police officer. My assumption was close – he earned his living as a security guard at the Legislature Building. When I met him, however, he was enjoying a family-style Saturday-afternoon shopping excursion. We chatted, rather aimlessly, it seemed at the time, while the people he was with browsed in the bookstore. It soon became apparent, however, that this man was not only interested in the phenomenon of ghosts, but was also quite knowledgeable about the paranormal field in general.

Alberta Legislature Building

"I can give you a generic palm reading," he commented casually. My response was anything but casual. I promptly thrust my hand in front of the man's face. He looked at it in silence for moment. When he began to speak he was amazingly accurate, detecting, among other things, a physical discomfort I was suffering at the time that I'd not mentioned to anyone. Also, to my great embarrassment, he described with amazing accuracy, a long-held secret.

Perhaps feeling uncomfortable about having revealed knowledge about something so personal to a total stranger, the man revealed a confidence of his own.

"There's a ghost at the Legislature Building," he stated flatly.

"Is there?" I asked with a hint of frustration in my voice.

"Absolutely," he confirmed, before asking, "Why does that surprise you?"

I explained in detail the rumours I'd heard years before and how, despite my best efforts at interviewing those I thought would have inside information, the story had disappointingly fizzled. He immediately offered an explanation as to why the Sergeant-at-Arms would have a different view of the situation than he did.

"Oscar Lacombe and his boys aren't in the building overnight," he replied. "It's not just the Ledge either, there's something about the grounds in front of the building that's really spooky too, but neither of those are anything compared to the Haultain Building."

This man, who had been a stranger just minutes before, was quickly becoming a valuable resource for me.

"Tell me about it," I prompted.

The man described how he and others working for the security company that is contracted to patrol the area frequently feel an unseen presence as they go about their rounds.

"You can't hear the footsteps, but occasionally you can actually see impressions, footprints, being made on the carpet in the hallways, either in front of or behind you," he explained, adding that knowing you're not alone—while not being able to see or hear the person you sense—can be an unnerving experience.

When these guards are inside the building they presume that unless there's another guard nearby, they are alone. Frequently, however, as they pass by one or more of the offices along the hallways, they can hear muffled sounds of conversations from within. Of course it is their job to check out anything unusual and they do. Mysteriously, however, when they unlock and open the door to the room the noises are coming from, the sounds stop and they are staring into an empty room—or at least an area that appears empty.

Public tours are offered regularly through the Legislature Building. During these excursions, guides share many of the interesting oddities about the building. People are generally fascinated by the enormous portraits of King George V and Queen Mary that hang in the portrait gallery. The eyes in the paintings appear to follow you where ever you go. Watching other adults respond to this phenomenon with giggles of delight is as much fun as the feeling that you yourself are being watched by an inanimate canvas.

Perhaps the all-time favourite stop on the tour, though, is the "magic spot." On an upper floor there is an area about a metre in circumference that possesses amazing auditory qualities. Standing in that location you can clearly hear conversations being carried on in even far corners of the mammoth building. Guides explain that the architectural features of the building have created an acoustical pipeline to that one particular area. My new informant also had additional information about this oddity.

"The magic spot they show on the tours is only the one that stays in one place. There are lots of others around the Ledge but they're rarely in the same location twice. You never know, as you're walking along the corridors, when you're suddenly going to be listening to a conversation from two floors away," he explained.

Remembering that at the outset of his story this engaging man had included the grounds in front of the Legislature Building and the Haultain Building immediately to the north of those grounds in the "haunted" category, I asked him to also tell me about them.

"The footsteps again, even when you're outside, you know there's someone walking right beside you. But nothing compares to being inside that Haultain Building. You never feel as though you're alone. There's always the sense that someone's with you and watching you," he said.

At this crucial point in our conversation the man's family approached and indicated they were ready to leave the mall. I asked the man his name and he gave me a very unusual answer—a moniker that I took to be a nickname, therefore not much help should I have tried to contact him again. Although that was disappointing, at least I finally had the ghost story that had eluded me the first time around.

I may not know my informant by his real name, but I think I do know the ghost's identity. I suspect it is the unsatisfied spirit of Sir Frederick Haultain that roams the halls of our government buildings. Haultain was premier of North-West Territories at the turn of the century. In 1905, when Alberta and Saskatchewan became provinces in their own right, many people, Haultain himself included, believed he should have been made premier of one of the new provinces. Unfortunately, while Haultain was a Conservative, the federal government of the day was Liberal and so was not inclined to agree with that opinion. Haultain went on to become Opposition leader in the newly established province of Saskatchewan.

When he was 49 years old, Frederick Haultain married for the first time. Although the union officially lasted for 32 years, it could not have been a happy marriage. Haultain dutifully supported his wife, the former Marian St Clair Castellain, and her daughter from a previous marriage, even though the couple never shared a home and only briefly during the marriage did they even live on the same continent.

Given the political and personal frustrations during his life and the areas where the ghostly presence is felt, it's not hard to imagine that the spirit might be that of Frederick Haultain. Perhaps he's still attending to unfinished business in and around the halls of Alberta's government.

And so, years after beginning my research, I think I may have solved the mystery of the Alberta Legislature Building's ghost story.

GOVERNMENT HOUSE
AND THE PROVINCIAL ARCHIVES

Government House now shares its grounds with the Provincial Museum and Archives, but when the sandstone residence was built in 1913, it stood alone, high on the north bank of the North Saskatchewan River. The imposing building was designed, in part, by Allan Jeffers, who also designed the Alberta Legislature Building. For twenty-five years the building served as the official residence of the province's lieutenant-governors. Since that time, the mansion has in turn been vacant, leased to an airline company and a veterans' home; today it is a venue for governmental conferences, meetings and formal dinners.

On January 1 each year, the public is invited to attend a reception at Government House. The roots of this gala, known as the Lieutenant-Governor's Levee, can be traced back an astounding 350 years. The gathering is a popular one. Albertans from all walks of life mingle with government officials, high-ranking members of the military and Mounties in their full-dress scarlet uniforms as they all enjoy light refreshments. By the time New Year's Day draws to a close, often nearly

Government House

a thousand people have been through the doors of the former residence.

The levee usually rates a small article in the following morning's newspaper. A ninety-one-year-old who had worked at the house when it was a veterans' home and had volunteered to help out at the levee in 1996 commented to the press that the building's ghosts were happy ones.

Upon investigation, it would seem that that assessment would have to have been made by a woman because Archie, the ghost of Government House, is partial to the ladies. Employee Judy Wilson had some amazing stories to tell about the mansion's resident ghost.

"We call him Archie, for Archives," she began. "He travels between here and the Archives." Although the spirit makes his presence known equally to both men and women, the women who sense him rarely report feeling the discomfort that the men do.

Some of the staff wonder if Archie's presence at Government House is connected with former Premier William Aberhart's government decision that such an official residence was undemocratic in principle. While that was the official reason given, it's fairly clear, from the perspective of hindsight, that the closure of the house had considerably less to do with anyone's sense of democracy than it did with retaliation.

The premier was extremely angry with John Bowen, lieutenant-governor at the time, for refusing to approval three bills that Aberhart's Social Credit government wanted to have passed into law.

No matter what the motivation on the legislators' part, Lieutenant-Governor Bowen was suddenly and unceremoniously removed from the luxurious residence that he had with great justification presumed he would be able to call his home for his entire stay in office. For this reason some of the staff today wonder if the ghost might be Bowen, returning to enjoy his stay at Government House into eternity.

"The caretakers can tell some amazing stories. One supervisor was terrified," Judy Wilson states.

When Wilson explains Archie's habits, it's no wonder he gives people a start. "Archie follows people," she elaborated.

Regular staff are used to working with the sense of a presence accompanying them. Relief workers, however, are often unaware of the extraordinary stories involving Government House and so are unprepared to deal with some of the strange sensations they can experience there.

One relief caretaker who had been working upstairs suddenly rushed to the main floor looking distraught. He reported that someone was watching him work up there and that he felt extremely uncomfortable. After calming down, the man returned to his duties for a moment only. This time when he rushed back downstairs he stated flatly that he couldn't work up there. From the periphery of his vision he thought he'd seen someone or something watching him from a corner of the room. That was clearly enough for him.

Archie doesn't often allow himself to be seen but on at least one occasion he was felt physically, when he touched someone's leg.

Whoever the spirit is seems to be pretty much carrying on with his own life and only intrudes on people's lives occasionally. Papers are heard being shuffled in empty rooms and the elevators will, every now and again, travel up and down seemingly of their own accord. The staff has learned to accept these day-to-day activities but even regular staff members are startled when chandeliers throughout the house begin to shake or when they hear, but don't see, a hand being slammed down on a desk.

Archie has even accompanied people outside Government House onto the grounds. This movement may be why the staff assumes the ghost in the Archives is the same one that haunts Government House. The spirit in the back storage stacks at the Archives has been seen only by security staff working the graveyard shift.

"They say he is dressed as though he might have been a clerk around the turn of the century," a reference archivist reported.

If he is indeed the same spirit as the one that haunts Government House, in the newer building Archie is apparently too involved with his nocturnal research to bother anyone. He just sits among the collections reading quietly and apparently contentedly.

Next year, when the newspapers record the success of the New Year's Day Levee, maybe they should increase the attendance figures by one in order to give Archie the attention and recognition he occasionally demands.

SISTER'S SPIRIT NURSES ON AT ST MICHAEL'S HOSPITAL

Lethbridge, in southern Alberta, is a particularly attractive city. Its location along the spectacular Oldman River valley is complemented by charming historic buildings mixed with striking modern architecture. Many of these attractive buildings, both old and new, are haunted. The most comforting and friendly of the Lethbridge ghosts is a nun who haunts St Michael's Health Centre.

Nurses have reported on several occasions that while they've been on their evening rounds patients have asked if the kindly nun who sat with them all through the previous night would be returning. This nun appears in a white habit and sits near the patients to offer them comfort while they are ill. No one has ever been able to identify the ghost. They've simply named her Sister.

Over the years only one patient ever complained of being frightened by seeing the ghostly presence. Any nurses who were initially spooked soon realized she was a good ghost, not a harmful one.

Elda Barva, a long-time administrator at the centre, recalls hearing about many instances when the apparition entered patients' rooms and was seen either by them or by nurses. A nurse who has also worked at St Michael's for a number of years and who asked to remain anonymous has encountered Sister on many occasions.

"One particular time I was working in ICU [intensive care unit]. There was a little hall and a phone in the hall and we had a back room where we kept the IV [intravenous] bags. Sister dropped one of the IV bags in front of the phone in the hallway. I put it back and she did it again," the nurse explained. After tidying up from this seemingly nonsensical prank several times the nurse noticed that, although there were dozens of intravenous bags in the room, only one was continually being set in front of the phone. Apparently the long-deceased sister's spirit wanted the bag thrown away—the expiration date marked on the bag had passed.

This particular trick of Sister's became an accepted warning to the staff at St Michael's. The ghost would take an IV bag from the room where it had been stored if it was outdated or if the hospital's supply of intravenous bags was running low.

On another occasion staff arrived at the hospital in the morning to find a fire hose draining into a bathtub. Upon thorough investigation there was no explanation as to who could have placed the hose in the tub, but the faucet the hose was attached to was found to be leaking. So, although there were puddles to be mopped up, the damage was considerably less severe than it could have been, only because an unseen presence moved the running hose from the hallway floor into the tub.

The ghost also warned the staff if patients needed help—by moving curtains, dropping items or giving some other sign. "We always paid attention," recalled the retired nurse. She added that on many occasions they would hear the elevator going up and down when there was no one in it.

"We knew Sister was doing her rounds," she affirmed. "She's taken temperatures, changed beds. She's a good ghost."

No one seems to know for sure whose spirit the ghost may be and it really doesn't matter much. What is evident is that the kindly woman's devotion to the sick and injured survived beyond her own death.

GRACE HOSPITAL

This story came to me in a rather unusual way. While attending a dinner meeting of the Alberta Historical Society, a friend and I shared a table with a couple we've chatted with on other occasions and a young man whom I had never met before. As we enjoyed the meal and one another's company, we exchanged information about what we did for a living. When I identified myself as the author of *Ghost Stories of Alberta*, the young man, Jon Dolphin, said that he and a friend had been collecting Alberta ghost stories in 1991. He indicated that he might still be able to turn up the stories and leads they'd collected if I would be at all interested in looking at them. This offer seemed too good to be true and I tried very hard not to get my hopes up. A few days after we'd been chatting, however, a bulky envelope arrived in my mailbox. The following intriguing tale was nestled in the cache.

As I don't know who recorded this story I have no way of knowing the writer's gender. I have, completely arbitrarily, inserted feminine pronouns.

The writer indicated that from 1982 to 1985 she worked at Grace Hospital. While allowing that such a building is bound to be full of unexplained noises, she was still convinced that at least one area of the hospital was haunted.

After reading her report, you might be convinced too. The haunted room is a delivery room in the maternity ward.

"It had been known for years that a woman in labour, placed in that particular room would have a long and difficult delivery, often ending in a Caesarean section. The nurses avoided placing patients in that room, unless the hospital census of the day dictated otherwise," the former employee explained.

Grace Hospital

The reputation of that one delivery room was so well accepted by hospital staff that when a patient in another ward declared himself to be a psychic he was invited to spend some time in the delivery room in question and report his findings to the staff.

"The psychic who read the room came out with this story: There was a ghost residing in that room. Her name was Maudine and she had died in childbirth many years ago. She feared that if she allowed a woman to give birth in that room, they would die as she had. Some of us believed this story, some of us didn't," the writer advised, while avoiding any explanation as to in which camp she belonged.

Many weeks later, the writer of this account was helping a young family to prepare to leave the hospital with their newborn infant. Just then the old Grace Hospital heating pipes began making a terrible racket. To the family, she quipped, "Oh, that's just our resident ghost, Maudine."

The new father looked at her in amazement.

"Maudine?" he asked. "Maudine Riley?"

Now it was the hospital employee's turn to be amazed. She'd never thought of the ghost as ever having had a last name. She listened intently as he explained that he was a direct descendant of the Riley family who had originally owned the land on which the hospital was built.

"The land adjacent to the hospital is still called Riley Park. The hospital is built on the site of the original Riley homestead," he told her.

Our informant must have been an amateur investigator because she turned up a photograph of the two-storey Riley home, long before it was demolished.

"The first floor consisted of kitchen and living space, the second floor of the bedrooms and maid's quarters. Maudine Riley lived in that house and died in childbirth in a second floor bedroom many years ago. In viewing the photo it became evident that the room where Maudine had died was almost in the exact same location where she now resided as a ghost," the informant detailed.

The Riley descendant told her that there had been a monument erected to the memory of Maudine and her baby at the Catholic church across the street from the hospital.

"I drove by the church that afternoon and saw the monument, like a grave marker, but was too afraid to get out of my car to see it. From that day on the ghost of Maudine was no joke to me and as far as I know, to this day, the delivery room nurses avoid putting labouring women in the room at the end of the hall," she concluded.

HOSPITAL VISITORS

My informant for the following stories has asked to be identified only as Virginia. Considering the dramatic content of her reports and that she is still associated with the hospital in which the incidents occurred, I could fully understand her request.

Virginia opened the conversation by saying that she knew for a fact that she wasn't the only nurse to have had unexplained and unexplainable encounters on the wards.

In the pediatrics area the call bell would occasionally ring in a room without a patient, or noises would be heard from an empty room. Staff would check and there'd be no one there. Once, however, there was an apparition seen. From the description, senior staff deduced it was the ghost of a former staff member.

"I remember a man working at the nursing station went down to a room to answer the call light. He came flying out of there and quit shortly after. He never told anyone why," Virginia recalled with a puzzled tone to her voice.

One night as she worked in the intensive care unit Virginia noted that an elderly woman's heart monitor alarm sounded.

"It should have registered a certain arrhythmia [prior to her death] but instead it just went flat. Of course, it could have been an equipment failure, I don't know. The patient's family were all at the hospital and so I went to tell them of the woman's death. As I went to where they were waiting I walked by an empty room," Virginia explained, remarking that the empty room was also equipped with a heart monitor although, of course, it wasn't hooked up. "As I passed the room that monitor suddenly registered the pattern that the recently deceased woman's monitor should have. I suspect it was the woman's soul passing through the empty room."

In another section of the hospital there is a "quiet room" where nurses working night shifts can rest.

"Whenever I went in there I left all the lights on. If I turned the lights off I felt as though there was someone sitting in a chair watching me. I never said anything to anyone about my feelings, though, until a new staff member announced that she would never go in there again. She felt someone had been bugging her. It seemed as though a child was trying to get her up, she told us."

Given the nature of hospitals, it shouldn't really be surprising that they can be the venue for paranormal experiences.

"There's always lots of talk of angels and the like," Virginia said. "Often if a patient who has been on a unit for quite a while dies, other patients and staff will still see the deceased. Another time a man said that someone came to him in the night to talk to him and comfort him."

Virginia doesn't know who the kindly soul might have been. She just knows that it wasn't a staff member and that there were no visitors on the ward that night—none that she could see, anyway.

One sighting was particularly dramatic because the patient who had the experience knew the name of his nocturnal visitor. It was the name of a patient who had died some time before. The two had never met!

And so life and death go on in our hospitals, under the watchful eyes of the hospital staff and the hospital ghosts.

AN UPDATE ON GEORGE BAILEY AND THE GALT MUSEUM

Not long ago I was invited to give a reading in Lethbridge. The evening's presentation was gratifyingly well attended and well received. It seems that many people in the south of our province are intrigued with the possibility of the existence of ghosts.

At the end of the evening a gentleman approached me and offered his name and phone number, with the ever-enticing rider, "I have a couple of stories I think you'll like."

He was certainly right.

A few years ago, Mike Prokop had been helping to research a project for the Galt Museum. The stately old building that houses the museum was originally a hospital and as such was the site of many deaths. Today it is widely accepted as being haunted and the ghost is generally believed to be that of George Bailey, an area farmer who died in the hospital in 1933 as a result of a freak accident. The unfortunate Mr Bailey had gone to the hospital with a broken leg and was being moved to the operating room in order to have the fracture set. The elevator doors malfunctioned and opened before the elevator was at the floor. Before he realized that the elevator wasn't there, an attendant had pushed Bailey's wheeled stretcher through the open doors and the man fell to his death down the empty shaft.

Now, more than sixty years later, the man's spirit remains. Bailey has made his presence known to many people over the years. At the Galt Museum's annual Halloween celebration, hundreds of people, including many of Bailey's descendants, come to hear the stories about Lethbridge's best-known ghost.

Mike Prokop, who has always had an open mind about these sorts of things, recounted a personal experience. Encountering George was certainly not on his mind one day when he and collection technician Richard Shockley went into the basement of the Galt Museum.

"I had noticed that some of the information [in the project] wasn't correct," he explained. "I suggested to Mr Shockley that we make the changes directly on the computer."

Mike presumed they were alone in the basement of the old building and so was startled when he heard footsteps.

"Did you hear that?" he asked.

As Richard had experienced George's presence himself on a few occasions, he knew just exactly what sounds Mike was referring to.

"It sounded like [someone walking in] stocking feet or slippers. We went along the corridor until we got to an area that was ice cold. There was something cold coming from the elevator shaft area but it wasn't a breeze. The hair on my neck stood straight up. I was uncomfortable."

Just listening to Mike's description of the incident gave me goose bumps because it was almost identical to the description Richard had given me when he had encountered the museum's resident ghost several years before. It seems that ever since his premature death, George Bailey has roamed the halls of the building in which he died. That old building has been added to over the years but, as with most spirits, Bailey has stayed within the realm in which he died, never venturing forth into the impressive new addition.

Mike was relieved to discover this peculiarity for himself the next time he was in the basement working with Richard.

"We were under the new addition and he got called away. I told him, "Don't leave me here alone," Mike explained, adding that he remembered only too well how unnerving the experience in the other part of

The Galt Museum

the basement had been. "But nothing happened." No doubt Richard had known Mike would be okay in this part of the basement.

"I had told my wife about the [first] experience," Mike told me. "I took her to the museum. In one room there was a display of hospital equipment. Lydia was pointing out a pair of forceps. The air around me seemed to get ice cold."

As he felt the hair on the back of his neck stand up, Mike was forced to acknowledge that he had probably just had his second encounter with the spirit of the long-deceased George Bailey. Oddly, the phantom didn't seem to disturb Lydia, who was standing right beside her husband.

Perhaps Lydia's lack of reaction only serves to prove that some people are more tuned to experiencing a ghostly encounter than others, a fact that George's descendants find endlessly disappointing, for they have told me they would enjoy meeting their eerie ancestor.

OKOTOKS TRAIN STATION

I was invited to give readings at both the high school and the junior high school in the town of Okotoks. Everywhere I went that day, teachers and students alike were telling me about the ghost in the Okotoks train station. The town's old train station, built in the 1920s, is no longer used for that purpose, but now serves as a cultural centre. Brenda Cupelli related the entire anecdote to me.

"I was the town's cultural co-ordinator from 1987 to 1988. I'm also a psychic, so I do encounter spirits, and [this spirit] wasn't a very nice one," Brenda explained. "She wore a long black dress with a bustle and a hat. Whenever trains came she would fly out of there [a small theatre] to [what is now] the art gallery. The gallery used to be the train station waiting room."

Brenda knew when the spirit was around because the long deceased woman's presence was foreshadowed by a high-pitched noise.

"I worked at night and every night it was a challenge. She'd stand over me. On a couple of occasions she walked right through me. I felt she was bitter and waiting for someone who had never come."

One day a woman was visiting the cultural centre with her little boy. The child headed off by himself toward the theatre while his mother and Brenda chatted.

"He came running out of there saying 'There's a lady in there,'" Brenda recalled. However, Brenda wasn't really surprised. "I saw her there always and I've also seen other people react to her image. I've seen them suddenly rush out [of the theatre]."

Bearing out the theory that some people are more inclined to be aware of presences from another dimension than other people are, the woman who took over the job from Brenda never reported any strange occurrences at the station. Of course it's possible that, like many people, she's just not anxious to discuss her unusual working conditions.

HERITAGE PARK'S
PRINCE HOUSE

Calgary's Heritage Park has many wonderfully haunted old buildings. While I was researching my earlier book on ghosts the park manager, Rick Smith, told me he had once had a picture of the ghost in the park's Prince House. Unfortunately, the snapshot had been lost. When Jacquie Dobson of Calgary told me that she also had a photograph of "the lady in white," one that wasn't lost, I was delighted.

The ghostly image was captured quite accidentally when Jacquie, her boyfriend, her sister, her son and her father were on an outing in September of 1992.

Jacquie's father took the two pictures, intending only to record his grandson's day at the park. As is clear from the boy's progress toward the house, the two shots were taken only seconds apart. In the first frame, grandson Jesse is approaching the front steps of the Prince House. There is an image at the window on the second floor immediately to the left (as you view the photograph) of the porch. In the second frame young Jesse has reached the porch and the image is gone.

When Jacquie first saw the two shots she was puzzled. "I tried to make sense of it. Shadows from the trees? The sun's reflections? Because the two pictures were taken so close in time and one picture had the [image] and one didn't I decided to look into the picture a little further. I took a magnifying glass, and I was amazed at what I was seeing."

Jacquie decided that this puzzle needed further investigation, so she took the picture to a photo shop and had it enlarged. The image started to make sense then.

"What I could see was the image of a lady in a long white gown, with her arms crossed as if holding something. After studying this picture for some time, I decided I wanted to see more, so I took the picture back to [the photo shop technician] and had him enlarge just the window. The details of this figure were more clear to me now. You can see the outline of this lady. Halfway in the bottom part of the window you can see her hand. You can see her fingers, and a ring on her ring fin-

The Prince House

ger of what looks like her right hand," Jacquie described, and then closed with a cryptic comment: "Well, you be the judge as to what you might see in these pictures."

A photograph of a ghost is very rare and to know of the same ghost being captured on film twice is really amazing. Perhaps the apparition at the Prince House is a bit of a ham and enjoys having her picture taken.

THE LOUGHEED HOUSE

"You'll find an article about the ghost on page 11 of the January 24, 1948, edition of the *Calgary Herald*," advised Trudy Cowan, President of the Lougheed House Conservation Society. Well, I'll admit that some weeks I'm a little late putting the recycling out, but even I don't have newspapers that old around the house. Fortunately the library at the university does, and so I was able to read the piece Trudy referred to.

Written in the decidedly insensitive journalistic style of the day, the anonymous reporter no doubt captured the readers' interest with the headline, "Girls Have Ghost." The scribe went on to tell of the apparition seen by Red Cross employees housed at the Lougheed House. The young women described "a woman in a white, flowing gown."

The article tells how Katharine Mackenzie, visiting Calgary from her native Montreal and working for the Red Cross, reported sleeping in her room on the top floor of the mansion. The sound of her bedroom door opening wakened her. Young Katharine then watched as the pale image of a woman "moved with grace about the room."

Katharine also commented that when the image was moving about, the floor in her room didn't squeak the way it normally did when someone walked on it. The apparition moved in complete silence. The sighting obviously didn't frighten the visitor from Montreal because she spoke to it. "But the form vanished without the courtesy of making any reply," according to the *Herald*'s article.

Patsy Ridout of Toronto, temporarily working and staying at the Lougheed House, confirmed Katharine's story with an experience of her own. Patsy went to sleep in her room with the door closed. She awoke to find it open. Patsy closed the door only to have it reopen, apparently of its own volition. The third time this happened, the apparition that Katharine had seen now became visible to Patsy, who showed amazing composure. The newspaper recorded that "realizing she was competing on unfavourable terms, she conceded victory, shrugged and went back to sleep."

If the image has been seen since, those sightings haven't been as well documented. Whose spirit was roaming around the Lougheed House those nights nearly fifty years ago is completely open to conjecture. When asked if she had any ideas who the ghost may have been Trudy Cowan simply said "no." Given the long and colourful history of the home, it's no wonder she was not willing to chose one possibility over any of the others.

"The first portion of the home was built in 1891 for James Lougheed and his wife, Isabelle Hardisty Lougheed. The family enlarged the home prior to World War I. Senator Lougheed lived there until his death in 1925, and the family had the home until Lady Lougheed's death in the 1930s," Trudy explained.

If the ghost was from the Lougheed's time in the beautiful old home, then it is possible that it was either Lady Lougheed or her one daughter who survived into adulthood. The numbers of women it housed after that, though, make speculation rather pointless. During the Depression the building was taken over to house a federal-provincial training program that taught young women the skills necessary to become home nurses and household staff. Hundreds of women stayed at the house during their training. Then, when the Second World War broke out, the Lougheed House served as a barracks for the Canadian Women's Army Corps.

Shortly after the war, the Red Cross bought the place for the princely sum of $10,000. It made good use of the place until 1979, when it was "bulging at the seams," according to reports Trudy Cowan has heard. The organization threatened to tear the old place down and build something more suitable to its purposes. Since the Red Cross owned the building, it could do as it pleased, but the province was vehemently opposed to demolition. The two parties negotiated an agreement whereby the Red Cross moved into more fitting premises and the Lougheed House was declared a historic site.

"It was designated a historic site by the province for its architectural and historic significance and more recently it was designated a national historic site for its architecture," Trudy Cowan indicated.

The mammoth project of restoring the home to its original grandeur is now well underway and soon the onetime home of Senator and Lady Lougheed (former Premier Peter Lougheed's grandparents) will be open to the public.

Even though Trudy's not willing to take a guess as to the ghost's identity, she doesn't seem to doubt her existence: "I think she's happy here with what we're doing. It just feels right."

FORT EDMONTON PARK'S FIRKINS HOUSE

Fort Edmonton Park is a living museum, a tribute to the area's history. Some of the buildings in Fort Edmonton Park are replicas, but others have been painstakingly moved from their original locations to the grounds of the park.

In 1992 a certain family offered to donate their house to the park. They planned to build a new home on their lot and felt the unique condition of the old storey-and-a-half building made it a historic resource too valuable to merely demolish. Park administrators agreed and gratefully accepted the couple's generous offer.

The house was one of many residences built along Saskatchewan Drive in 1911 for faculty at the nearby University of Alberta. Over the years, fate and the wrecker's ball have claimed all but a few of the original houses. Those that remain have, understandably, been renovated and modernized on many occasions throughout their existence. After all, not many families are content to live with the disadvantages presented by antiquated plumbing, heating, insulation, electricity and the like.

What made this particular family's offer to Fort Edmonton so valuable is that no renovations had ever been done on the eighty-one-year-old building. From both the inside and the outside of this house, it appeared as though time had stood still. This state of affairs would have been astonishing enough if only one family had ever occupied the residence, but this family was in fact the fifth owner.

And so, the Firkins house, named for its first owners, arrived at its new site in the park complete with the original steam heat radiators, creaky staircase, shallow porcelain kitchen sink, badly sloping porch...and resident ghost.

The most recent owner spoke candidly with park staff about the phantom that would, no doubt, come along with the house. Over the years the couple had been aware of a ghostly presence. One morning, as the woman of the couple came down the staircase, she clearly saw the image of a young man sitting at her dining-room table. Another time she's sure the ghost jumped on her back.

Stories from former residents include one in which a male voice was heard singing lullabies to an infant who smiled, cooed contentedly and then obligingly fell asleep in response to the song. Every time the child's mother went up the stairs to check on the sounds, they stopped abruptly. The woman reported that she didn't feel the music or its source were cause for concern because the child was so clearly soothed by them.

The apparition is generally believed to have been the son of a former owner of the house. Apparently the young man died while living in the house and his spirit still roams the residence.

From the moment the house arrived at Fort Edmonton, it has been apparent that the entity made the trip with the house. And, based on the goings-on since the house has been moved from its lot overlooking Edmonton's river valley, it's probably safe to assume that the young man's spirit is not entirely happy with the change in venue.

The door to the back bedroom, which was open when the move began, stood closed when the building reached the site set aside for it in the park. It remained unopenable even after specially trained workers lowered the house to its level foundation. Finally, workers removed the latch mechanism and pried the stubborn door open. Strange to note, the door swung freely then, giving no indication of what might have jammed it. The lock on the door, workers noted with great interest, had been painted over years ago.

Furthermore, before the trip to the park began, workers had locked all the windows in the house. But, upon arrival at Fort Edmonton, the windows stood wide open. It's highly unlikely that all of the locks could have become unlatched on their own during the journey.

Given the nature of their jobs, the employees at Fort Edmonton Park are accustomed to working in creaky old buildings, and yet many report feelings of uneasiness while working in the Firkins house.

It was a relief to administration staff at the park when they returned a music box they discovered in the house. While the device sat on the corner of communications officer Jan Repp's desk, it would play a note whenever anyone came near it.

It will be interesting to see how the ghost in the Firkins House reacts to all his visitors.

CHAPTER 4

THE SPIRIT'S INN

THE DEANE HOUSE

I was delighted to be asked to speak at the October 1994 meeting of the Alberta Historical Society's Calgary chapter, and doubly pleased when I heard the invitation included dinner at the Deane House for a guest and myself. My older daughter accompanied me that evening and, although we always enjoy ourselves there, we had no idea just how interesting this particular visit would be. Note that you don't have to be a haunted-house buff to enjoy a visit to the Deane House, because the restaurant is in a recently added part of the historic building and is not at all haunted.

Just before dinner, we were ushered to a table where five other members of the society were already seated. There was barely time for introductions before a short address from one of the executive members, and then dinner was served. I hadn't explained to our table mates why I was attending the function and they seemed quite surprised when, between the main course and dessert, I was asked to do a reading from my first book of Alberta ghost stories. Of course I chose to read the Deane House story and, just as predictably, our dessert conversation centred around the ghosts in the place.

"I've had an experience with a ghost here. I think I have a photograph of one of the ghosts," calmly stated Jacquie Dobson, the young woman seated across from me.

Her comment was followed by complete silence from the rest of us at the table. She may have wondered if we were all questioning her sanity. I wasn't—I was simply fascinated beyond words. Photographs of ghosts are decidedly rare phenomena.

As Jacquie related the events that led up to the photo being taken, Andre, her escort, excused himself and left the table. As he'd already described himself as a skeptic, I wondered if he wished to avoid such discussions. Seconds later I was so embroiled in Jacquie's tale that I never gave the man's disappearance another thought.

Jacquie explained that she and her sister, Christina, had long been intrigued by the phenomenon of ghosts. On the day that this picture was taken, the two sisters, accompanied by Andre, decided to have lunch at the Deane House. They were well aware of its haunted status – for Jacquie and Christina that was part of the appeal.

"We enjoyed our lunch and our conversation with our waitress. She was very open about her ghostly experiences in the Deane House. Christina had brought her camera, so after our lunch we took a tour of the house. As we toured, my sister took a variety of pictures," Jacquie recalled. "We made our way up to the attic. As we walked up the stairs, I got a real strange feeling. It was just an uneasy feeling. Christina continued to take pictures as Andre and I looked around."

The Deane House has dormer style windows in the attic, and one has storage closets on both sides. The closet on the right is full of paraphernalia while the one on the left is empty. Many years ago, Kerklan Hilton, communications co-ordinator at the time, explained to me, "The spirits don't like us to store anything in this closet. They become very agitated and so we respect their wishes."

This remark is especially interesting because the closet on the left looks exactly like the other one, except for a deep red stain that years of cleaning has not removed.

Jacquie and her two companions began investigating the attic area and noticed the stain. Andre, the skeptic, said mockingly, "Oh, look. There is blood on the floor."

The response from Jacquie was immediate and dramatic. The strange feelings she'd been experiencing as they explored the attic intensified. She quickly closed the closet door. Little did she know that mere minutes later her unidentifiable feelings were to increase enormously.

"There is a rocking chair in the attic. I decided to sit in it. As I sat in the chair, I felt really strange. I looked at my sister and told her I felt as though I was sitting on someone. She took a picture of me sitting in the rocker and as she did, Christina said her camera didn't seem to be working right," Jacquie explained. "She said it almost sounded as if the shutter went in slow motion."

Just at that second Jacquie felt something touch the back of her leg.

"I was so startled, I jumped out of the chair and ran behind my sister and Andre. I have to admit I was scared. I tried to explain to

The Deane House

Christina and Andre what had happened, but I was so scared I couldn't talk straight. I had tears in my eyes. That's when we decided to leave."

Whatever was in the attic was clearly more attracted to Jacquie than to either Andre or Christina.

"We were walking back down the stairs and the rocking chair continued to rock. Christina took some more pictures as we were leaving and found her camera to be working fine."

As they drove home, Jacquie calmed down sufficiently to talk about what she'd been feeling as she sat in the rocking chair. Even Andre admitted he felt a little strange while they were on the third floor of the Deane House.

"I told Christina to get that film developed right away, that I was certain there would be something on that one picture. I called my sister every day for three weeks, nagging her to get the pictures back," Jacquie told me.

"She finally got them back and I was not surprised at what I saw. You can see a long hand around me coming around my right side, another hand around the left side of my head and what looks like a head to the right of my head. So what it looks like is, I was sitting on someone and [that person] was reaching around me," she described.

The most interesting point of all, though, has to be the reflection in the mirror behind the rocking chair. It does not reflect what it should. The camera clearly captures the essence of something or someone between the rocking chair and the mirror. Something or someone that three pairs of eyes hadn't seen.

The experience that afternoon, coupled with the very strange photograph, went a long way towards convincing Andre that "maybe there is such a thing as ghosts." His attendance with Jacquie at the Deane House dinner the evening of my reading fully two years after their encounter with the spirits was certainly one clue that the experience at least heightened his curiosity. The other indication of a change in his attitude is that when Andre left the supper table unexpectedly, it was to drive home to get the picture that Jacquie had described. He wanted us to be able to see for ourselves. That photo is reproduced here (p. 138).

I have also heard from a woman who saw someone apparently go into the ladies' rest room just ahead of her. When she entered the room only seconds later, there was no one in sight—the woman had vanished. It seems there's always something new at Calgary's Deane House—or should that be something very old?

A Calgary firm, Shadow Productions, puts on "Murder Mystery" performances at the Deane House. Actors and crew alike have come to expect the unexpected during those presentations. They report that lights will frequently turn off when there's no one near the light switch and that doors will close when they shouldn't.

One member of the firm has a photo showing an image of a woman at a third-floor window—not an unusual possession except that when the photo was taken, the house was locked and empty. In addition, the cast has sometimes smelled pipe smoke coming from the room to the right of the front door. A man met a peaceful end in that room many years ago. Apparently during his life he enjoyed sitting in there and smoking his pipe. His image is still occasionally seen, as is a lady in the attic.

In yet another incident, a woman working for Shadow Productions got the scare of her life when she went into the basement of the Deane

House to change her clothes. She was greeted by the image of an old Indian brave.

Drop into the Deane House for lunch. The atmosphere's great, the food's delicious and you never know who you're going to see!

MRS CROSS HAS NEVER LEFT HER HOME

The stately old Cross House at 1240 8th Avenue SE in Calgary is now a delightful restaurant—but it began life as the Cross family home. Albert Ernest Cross was a wealthy and influential person during the City of Calgary's earliest days. He was one of the "Big Four" entrepreneurs (along with Pat Burns, George Lane and Archie McLean) responsible for establishing the world-famous Calgary Stampede. A substantial percentage of the money he used to help float the pioneer rodeo was revenue generated by his principal business interest, the Calgary Brewing and Malting Company.

The brewery was so important to Cross that, despite the unpleasant odours often associated with the fermentation process, he chose to build a grand home for his family within easy walking distance of the distillery—a small, but significant detail for the ghost story to follow.

A.E. Cross and his generation of the family have all been deceased for decades. Nevertheless, George Diamant, the personable general manager of the Cross House Garden Cafe, and some of his staff are not convinced that the original occupants have all left the elegant residence.

George recalled finishing work one evening after preparing for the following day's opening. Just as he and another employee were securing the back door, they both heard a chair being scraped across the hardwood floor upstairs. George and his co-worker, Catherine, looked at one another in disbelief for a moment before deciding they must accidentally have locked someone into the restaurant. They headed back

The Cross House

upstairs, George by the front staircase and Catherine by the back one. They met in the second floor hallway and proceeded together to the room where they'd heard the noise.

As far as they could see there was no one in the room, but two of the chairs at a carefully set table for five had been moved. Now, instead of being pushed up against a round table near the bay window, they stood away from the table, facing out the window. Both George and Catherine knew they hadn't left them that way and they also knew the chairs being moved must have made the sound they had heard as they were locking up. Still convinced that they'd mistakenly locked some-one into the restaurant, the puzzled co-workers searched the entire house. "We checked the place thoroughly and there was no one there," George recalled.

A few days later, Mary Cross Dover, Mr and Mrs Cross's daughter (now deceased), dropped into her former home to visit and enjoy lunch. Inevitably, she and George Diamant began chatting. The inci-dent with the chairs was still very much on the man's mind and, as gen-tly as he could, he steered their conversation around to the occur-rence. As he'd hoped she would, Mary was able to shed some light on the mystery.

The area where George and Catherine had discovered the chairs moved had been the home's master bedroom. Mary remembered that her mother would go up to the bedroom at about the time she expected her husband would be leaving his brewery each evening. She would pull a chair over to the bay window, which faced her husband's place of business. There she would sit, watching out the window, waiting to see him walking home each night. As soon as he came into view, Helen Cross would go down to the kitchen and begin dinner preparations.

That anecdote, George felt, explained the odd occurrence. He added that while Mrs Cross has never made her presence felt when anyone was around, every now and again, through small pranks, she reminds the staff that she hasn't left her beautiful old home. She enjoys moving chairs about after the staff has set them in place and occasionally cutlery settings will be shuffled around on tables.

George evidently takes great pleasure, not only in managing the Cross House, but in his association with Calgary history. And why not? There aren't many people who can claim they have to rearrange furniture or silverware moved by a pioneer, or at least by the ghost of one! Richard Praud has, perhaps, an even more dramatic story to tell about working with the Cross family's ghosts.

"It was 1967 and I had a young family to support. I was driving a cab...evenings and weekends, to make some extra money. One evening in the spring I was parked outside the York Hotel at Centre Street and Seventh Avenue. It was about 11:30. In those days everything shut down then and we [cab drivers] got what we called the big beer rush."

Praud must have been glad that he'd waited there long enough to be the first cab in line when 11:30 arrived, because there weren't too many customers that night.

"A man came out of the hotel. He was dressed all in black—even a black cowboy hat. He popped in [to the cab] and never said a word."

The part-time cab driver had no idea he was in for the fare of a lifetime. Even the man's silence didn't strike Richard as being odd.

"Lots of people wouldn't speak to you. This guy just pointed his finger and somehow I knew where he wanted to go."

When they arrived at the large, white corner house, Richard didn't pay too much attention to it. "I didn't know this was the Cross House, frankly I'd never even heard of A.E. Cross. The man paid me the fare—I think it was a $1.50, you must remember this was thirty years ago," the former driver cautioned. "I put the money away and looked up. The man in black was at the gate. I turned the light on inside the cab to write up my trip and he was gone. Again, though, I didn't think too much of it at the time."

Toward the end of his shift, Richard was tallying up his money against his trip record and he discovered that he was short by $1.50. Driving a silent passenger dressed in black who disappeared into thin air didn't disturb Richard Praud, but he was moonlighting to earn extra cash, so finding his balance sheet short at the end of a night was cause for concern.

"I'm a very meticulous kind of guy," he stated. "I always balanced my money, but this particular night I went over it and over it. No matter what I did I came out short," he remembers.

Eventually Richard gave up and tried to accept the fact that he had somehow been shorted. "I never gave it much thought after that," he said.

As it was 1967, Canada's centennial year, the Praud family, like many other Canadian families, began to develop an interest in their heritage.

"One day that summer my wife, Lynn, and I took our two daughters, Sandy and Mandy, to the Horseman's Hall of Fame. There was an exhibit about Calgary's Big Four and that's when I realized. I said to Lynn, "I drove that guy.""

Lynn Praud must have been very puzzled by her husband's comment for she could clearly see that the man whose likeness he'd pointed to had died on March 10, 1932, years before her husband had even been born. It was then, finally, that Richard Praud was able to piece together his strange experience of a few weeks before.

"You know, even at the time when I saw the guy, he looked too clean, too perfect. His skin was just too perfect. He looked like someone had cleaned him up for television," Richard recalled.

It was then, too that the former cab driver realized why his fare tally had been short by $1.50 that night. It was the long-deceased Mr Cross's fare that he was missing—on a spring night during Canada's centennial year, Richard Praud had taken a ghost for a drive.

CASPER THE VERY FRIENDLY GHOST

For four years in a row, Edmonton's La Casa Ticino restaurant has been rated as having the best atmosphere. In a city overpopulated with eateries, that distinction means a place must have something extra going for it. La Casa Ticino does—maybe more than many of its patrons realize.

In the 1930s the charming old house that is now home to the award-winning restaurant was the Casper family's home. It's a fair guess that at least one of the Caspers enjoyed living in the house so much that he or she still hasn't left. There's certainly nothing to be frightened of in this haunted house-cum-restaurant—the ghost is so friendly that once it even got fresh with one of the waiters. "Casper the Friendly Ghost" may be more than just a cartoon!

Darwin Christensen remembers his first exposure to the resident spirit at La Casa Ticino. It was a Friday evening in December 1995.

"I didn't even know I'd seen it until after, when I was talking to another waiter. That night it was really busy. We were just hopping," the personable young man explained.

In an attempt to get ahead of the rush a bit, Darwin took advantage of a quiet moment to roll cutlery into napkins in preparation for re-setting tables as they came available. Suddenly a ball of energy rushed behind him.

La Casa Ticino Restaurant

"It was such a big motion that I got a little churn in my stomach, but I kind of brushed it off because we were so busy. I just thought I was over-tired or something," Darwin told me. "I only remembered it later on when another waiter was talking about her experiences. She said it always got her as a rushing motion that you catch with your peripheral vision and it instantly grabs your attention. You can't help but notice it. I mean, you know there's something but when you look around there's nothing there."

The ball of energy always takes the same route, rushing toward a table for two situated under a small window. Both staff members who have experienced the strange apparition agree that it is about the height and colour of a black lab dog.

Darwin's next encounter with the phantom demonstrated that a ghost can be entirely too friendly. It happened on a Sunday.

"It was busy for just one waiter," he described. "I'd had several tables and I was just cleaning up after my rush. There were maybe ten other people in the room. I was bending over and I put the tray down [on the table]. I was filling it up with all the things from the table and a hand grabbed me from behind. It was firm like a hand, it wasn't like something had just brushed against me or my trousers had slid or anything like that, a hand grabbed me on the left side. I turned around thinking "Buddy, if you want something, why don't you just call me?" but there was no one there."

That's when Darwin realized he was standing at the table where the phantom rush of energy always headed. Although he certainly can't explain being touched, Darwin does have a theory that may explain the unusual presence in the old house.

"There may have been a bed where that table is now because [when the house was lived in] there were bedrooms on that top level. I was thinking that as the object was about the same height as a bed, maybe someone was bedridden for a long time."

Darwin is not the only member of the staff to have had strange experiences in La Casa Ticino. A woman who has since gone on to other employment told Darwin about locking the place up late one night. The restaurant's kitchen is an addition at the back of the old house. It is located halfway between the first and second floors. As the woman was preparing to leave the restaurant she heard a tremendous crash.

"The crash was so loud that she thought the entire kitchen had just dropped in the back," Darwin recalled. "She went rushing to the kitchen but nothing was even out of place."

As she was already aware of the rushing ball of energy, she was not entirely surprised. She merely continued the locking-up process, setting the appropriate alarms and locking the doors before leaving.

Gary Strangeway, La Casa Ticino's owner, listens to his employees' stories of the resident ghost with obvious interest but so far hasn't had an experience of that kind himself. He's just happy to have purchased a restaurant with such a great atmosphere, even if he can't take all the credit for it.

WHO COULD SHE BE?
LA BOHEME RESTAURANT

One day early in the spring of 1995, I was waiting for a friend to join me for an annual luncheon celebration. It's become traditional to hold this yearly ritual at La Boheme, a restaurant in a charming old building in the Highlands area of Edmonton. I arrived a bit earlier than our planned meeting time, so Ernst Eder, the restaurateur, showed me to a quiet table and offered me a cup of coffee while I waited.

The lunch crowd hadn't arrived yet and I decided to take advantage of what I knew would only be a temporary lull. As Ernst poured my coffee, I mustered up what I hoped was a casual-sounding voice and said, "This building's really old, isn't it? Would you happen to know if it might be haunted?"

The words were no sooner out of my mouth when the lid of the sugar dish at my table lifted off its base and set itself down on the table a good centimetre or more away from the bowl. I was grateful that Ernst was still standing beside me and so had also seen the strange movement. At least I knew that if I was seeing things, I wasn't alone in what I was seeing. And we both realized that my question had been answered on his behalf by the spirit herself.

After exchanging incredulous looks, followed by somewhat unnerved smiles, we continued our attempt at conversation.

"Oh, yes," Ernst confirmed, somewhat unnecessarily now. "She usually only comes out late at night, though, after closing."

As Ernst made that comment, the restaurant's hungry lunch-time crowd, my friend among them, began to arrive, effectively ending my opportunity to probe further for the story. I replaced the lid on the sugar bowl and went on to have a pleasant lunch. I put the incident at La Boheme pretty much out of my mind until a local librarians' association asked me to do a reading at one of their meetings.

"We're holding the meeting at La Boheme," the contact person advised me. I would have been delighted to accept the invitation no matter where the gathering was to be held, but I was even more pleased to have an opportunity to follow up on the unfinished ghost-hunting business from several months before.

It was a cold winter's night and Ernst Eder's warm greeting in the foyer of the restaurant was most welcome. As he hung up my coat, I decided that in order to avoid another missed opportunity I'd better launch into my questions and my reasons for them as quickly as I could. I introduced myself and reminded him of the incident with the sugar bowl lid.

"Would you be willing to share the story of La Boheme's ghost with me for my next book?" I asked.

After only a moment's hesitation, he kindly agreed. The building, officially known as the Gibbard Block, was constructed in 1913 as a luxury apartment building. The spirit likely lived or worked in the building during its early days. She is a distinctly benign spirit who rarely makes herself felt while the restaurant is open.

"When the staff's closing up at night, though, they can sometimes hear her and feel her presence. Other than that she stays in the basement," Ernst explained.

For this reason, the staff suspects the phantom may have been a laundress for one of the original families who lived in the apartment building. Over the years, a few staff members have told Ernst that they feel uneasy if they're alone in the restaurant late at night. Some have gone so far as to ask that they not be scheduled to lock up. The restaurateur has always been happy to comply with those requests. Despite his apparent understanding of the occasional staff member's unease, it's clear that Ernst Eder enjoys La Boheme just as much as its resident spirit does.

THE GHOST TAKES A BATH

Not long ago, I was invited to Lethbridge to do some readings and interviews. Everyone was always so welcoming wherever I went in the city that when a camera operator for *The Rene Newhouse Show* began chatting with me before the program, I wasn't surprised. Seconds before I was to go on, the woman gave me her phone number on a slip of paper along with this cryptic message: "Call me. I have a story I think you'll like."

Well, I finally made that call and I'm certainly glad that I did. Despite the number of provocative ghost stories I've heard over the years, a few really stand out as being especially eerie. Jean Van Kleek's story is one of those.

In 1976, Jean was supporting herself as a musician. "I sang and played the guitar and keyboard," she explained. Constant travel is an accepted part of such a life and so the young woman was well accustomed to staying in motels and hotels around the province.

"It was usually midnight by the time I got to my room. I had a habit of always putting the extra latch on when I locked the door at night," she remembered.

During a week's stay in Taber, however, Jean had a little trouble with the extra locking mechanism.

"When I woke up the first morning, the latch was off the door. I was very annoyed with myself. I could hardly believe that I'd have forgotten to lock it."

By the end of her stay in Taber, she knew the lack of security couldn't be blamed on her absent-mindedness. It turned out that the lock problem was only the first event in what was to be an unforgettable week.

"The next night when I got into my room, I was doubly conscious to lock the door, latch and all. Before I went to bed I checked again and so I knew for sure that the latch was on. When I woke up in the morning, it was off again. The only thing I could figure was that for some reason I'd gotten up in the middle of the night and unlatched it. This was really an odd thought to me because I'd never sleepwalked before in my life."

The third night in the room, Jean again dutifully locked herself in, but rather than go right to bed, she decided to stay up and watch some television.

"That's when I heard it," she said quietly. "Water swishing in the bathtub. That's a very distinctive sound, not one you'd confuse with anything else. And it was clearly coming from the bathroom adjoining my room."

Momentarily frozen in horror, Jean soon realized she would have no choice but to go into the bathroom, confront whoever was in there and explain as calmly as possible that he or she had gotten into the wrong hotel room.

"I knew it was going to be embarrassing," she recalled. "But I also knew it had to be done. I screwed up my courage, walked into the bathroom and looked over at the tub. I couldn't believe my eyes. The bathtub was completely empty. There was no one in the room and no water in the tub."

The irony then was that Jean was more concerned by the fact that the bathroom was empty than she had been when she was sure someone was in there. She knew what she'd heard and where it had come from even though there was no apparent explanation for the noises. Showing amazing calmness, Jean turned in a little later and slept soundly through the night. The next morning all was quiet but once again the security latch had been taken off the door.

Jean's contract to provide the musical entertainment for the hotel's lounge specified that she had to stay another three nights. "Every night at the same time I heard the sounds of swishing water coming from the bathtub and every morning the latch was off the door," she stated. Then she added, "When I checked out, the desk clerk seemed a bit surprised. He said something like, 'They gave you THAT room?' I said 'yes' and asked why that would surprise him. He told me, 'It's just that we don't usually rent that room. A guy died in there a while ago. He had a heart attack while he was taking a bath.'"

Now at least Jean had an explanation for the strange events she'd been witness to over the past week. I asked whether or not she'd been frightened by her encounter and she replied, "It wasn't really a bad feeling, it was just a 'there' feeling."

Jean's hunch that I'd enjoy hearing her eerie anecdote was certainly accurate. Few stories have chilled me quite as effectively as hers did.

BLACK CAT RANCH

The January 1993 edition of the Writers' Guild of Alberta newsletter carried a short article about a writers' retreat that had been held at the Black Cat Ranch, just outside Hinton, some weeks before. A storm had caused a power failure at the ranch during the weekend getaway, re-sulting in a group of wordsmiths being huddled together in a dark-ened lodge listening to the wind wail outside. The inevitable result was an evening of ghost stories. In the article, reference was made to the "Black Cat ghost" and a "haunted room."

I may have missed the retreat but I couldn't miss the ghost story. I called Amber Hayward, fellow writer and part owner of the Black Cat, and asked her to share the story for this book.

"You should talk to my mother," Amber replied. "She's the one who saw the ghost."

Mary Bond, Amber's mother, was disarmingly matter-of-fact about her strange encounter with the apparition.

"It was the summer of 1976 and we were building a new lodge. We had a portable generator for power. One day I wanted to do dishes so I needed power and walked over to the construction site. I looked into the foundation. It was nearly 2 metres deep at that point. There was a big man standing there [in the foundation]. He could not possibly have gotten down there without a ladder, not a man that big," Mary began.

As both Mary's husband and son-in-law were at a different part of the site that day, they had the ladder with them.

Part of the charm of the Black Cat Ranch is that it is secluded. With directions it is simple enough to find, but it's highly unlikely anyone would just happen upon that particular location, let alone find it and then jump into a 2 metre deep construction pit.

Assuming that the man was there to see either her husband or her son-in-law, Mary simply went on about her work. That evening, however, she asked her husband, "Who was your visitor?"

He replied, "What visitor?"

Mary described the man she'd seen that afternoon but the description meant nothing to her husband. Further, he assured her there hadn't been any man, of any description, visiting the site at any point that day.

Puzzled by the contradiction between what she knew she had seen and her husband's assurances that no one had been there, Mary made a point to return the next day at exactly the same time to the place where she'd seen the man. Despite the fact that she was well used to the appearance of the excavation Mary hoped the second trip would prove that what she'd thought she'd seen had merely been an optical illusion. It proved nothing of the sort.

"There were no shadows," she recalled.

Who, then, could the apparition have been? Of course, there's no way to know for sure, but Mary has a theory that is connected to the history of the area. Local legends tell of male Crees who once walked from what is now Ontario all the way to the Rocky Mountain foothills, where the Black Cat Ranch is located. Some of those travellers settled in the area and were eventually buried there, too. Mary Bond believes that the ghost she saw may have been one of that group. Perhaps the apparition was merely curious about what Mary's family was doing with the land he had settled on so many years before.

The Hotel Macdonald

HORSE HAUNTS THE MAC

The year was 1915 and Edmonton's economy boomed. Everyone, it seemed, was making money, especially the railways. In order to capitalize on this financial good fortune, the Grand Trunk Pacific Railway built a truly spectacular hotel on a prime piece of Edmonton real estate. The huge lot abutted the downtown business section and overlooked the North Saskatchewan River valley. The railway named its impressive inn after Canada's first prime minister.

At its opening, the Hotel Macdonald was acknowledged to be one of the most elegant lodging houses in western Canada. Sadly, the years were not kind to "the Mac." Its splendour suffered badly and by the time the hotel closed its doors in 1983, the once-proud Edmonton landmark was badly down at its heels.

Today the hotel is owned by Canadian Pacific Hotels and Resorts. After the company's investment of nearly $30 million in renovations, it is once again one of the world's great hotels. The Mac serves as a luxurious home-away-from-home for the rich, the famous and those who enjoy being pampered and surrounded by grandeur.

Despite all these changes, the slow decline, the years of abandonment, the massive renovations and now the re-entry into the field of luxurious accommodations, at least one ghost has remained in residence.

The story goes that in 1915 horses were used to haul away the earth from the original excavation. One horse apparently died on the job. The staff occasionally report that when they are in the basement of the hotel they can hear the clip-clopping sound of horse's hooves as the long-dead animal labours on into eternity.

There is, however, at least the rumour of a second ghost at the Hotel Macdonald. The administration won't verify the story but many people have told me about a laundry worker from the hotel's early days. Rumour has it that the man met an untimely death at the hotel and that his spirit has stayed on. The widespread rumour and the hotel's official denial make a tantalizing combination.

THE WELL-HAUNTED PRINCE OF WALES HOTEL

The Prince of Wales Hotel in Waterton National Park dates back to the 1920s. When it opened, the price of a night's accommodation was just less than $10. Many people felt that the rate was excessive, but those who could afford to do so happily paid the price for the privilege of being surrounded by the park's striking geography and pampered by the attentive staff at the luxurious hotel.

Two women, both former employees at the Prince of Wales, have felt such an affinity for the place that they seem to have taken up residence on a permanent basis. So far, one has stayed for over fifty years and the other one for twenty.

A young man, whom we shall call Joe, was involved in a re-roofing project at the hotel. He had quite a story to tell about his encounters with the older of the two spirits and her influence over these renovations. Part of Joe's responsibilities included taking detailed measurements and assessing what materials would be required to bring each room up to standard. All the rooms were on the west side of the hotel, but spread from the second to the sixth floors.

"These rooms had been vacant for a number of years but the proprietors thought they could redo [them] and make them available for guests," Joe explained, and then added, "It was on the sixth floor that I first encountered the strangeness that still leaves me baffled."

Joe described the rooms on the sixth floor as being in four groups of four. "I was measuring rooms in the northwest quadrant when I heard a door slam. There was no one else up at that level. The regular maintenance staff was down on level one and the roofers were outside. I didn't think anything about it at the time, attributing the door closure to the wind. The Prince of Wales is an old building and drafty so a door closing could easily have been [caused] by the wind," Joe assured me.

He finished up where he was and prepared to repeat the process in the next room—the room with the now-closed door.

"Somehow the door had locked upon closing. I had to walk down six levels to find a maintenance person, get keys from him, and walk back up to the sixth. When I got back [to the room] the door was open," Joe reported. "There was no one about. I walked into the room. It was cold, much colder than the adjacent rooms."

Remarkably, though by now Joe recognized that he was dealing with extraordinary circumstances, his next actions were as follows: "It wasn't that I was afraid, but curious, about what was going on. I sat down in the room.... The temperature in the room got warmer and with it a sense of injustice done in the room permeated my thinking. After I had 'communicated' with the strangeness, I went about my work and left the room."

Still curious about what might have caused his experience, Joe began subtly probing the hotel staff for information. It was then that he heard something about a ghost in the hotel. "Although the reports seemed to indicate the entity moved about the hotel, for the most part the reports centred around the northwest corner," he told me. Of course that was the area in which Joe had encountered the strangeness he experienced.

"Legend had it that a murder took place up in that area shortly after the Second World War. The upper levels of the hotel [at that time] were given over to staff," he said. "One of the cooks and his wife lived in the area in question. She was a vivacious, outgoing, friendly concierge. He was an extremely jealous person. One Friday night after she returned to their room after spending a few hours playing cards with other staff, her husband, in a fit of rage, killed her."

The husband then fled from the couple's quarters, having locked the door behind himself. Just as he had no doubt hoped, his wife's body was not found until Monday. By then he must have put considerable distance between himself and the corpse, because he was never caught. Joe was told that the hotel staff now believe the banging doors and creaking noises are attempts by the deceased to draw attention to this grievous injustice.

While Joe was carrying out his duties inside, other workers were labouring on the roof of the hotel.

"They were [working] on an area of the roof that was over the room in question. This section was proving tougher to get through than the rest. The workers' nails tended to bend and shingles were slipping from their hands. They attributed it to frost, wind and harder than normal wood," Joe explained. "I took a different approach. I went back inside and climbed up the six floors to the room [with the door] that had slammed shut on me. I entered the room and in a calm voice talked to the room. I said that by letting the roofers pound their nails in and hold on to their shingles they would be away from the area quicker and peace would follow. I felt something that I can't describe and [then I] left the room. I returned outside and when the roofers came down I asked them how things were going. They said that for some inexplicable reason the nails were not being bent and the shingles were not slipping from their grasp. They made record time on that portion of the roof and were on to other sections."

The other spirit at the hotel is Sarah. She's an apparition who is actually still seen occasionally by staff at the Prince of Wales Hotel. As a teenager, Sarah worked at the facility. She apparently had a schoolgirl

The Prince of Wales Hotel

crush on a fellow employee—an executive with the hotel. Her feelings were not reciprocated and the result was tragic – the youngster jumped to her death from the hotel's seven-storey-high bell tower.

One guest I spoke with reported that he and his wife could feel, although not see, someone tucking them into their bed the nights they stayed there. He also commented that no matter how many times he opened the window, when he woke up it was closed and locked. The man assured me that he had no history of sleepwalking and that his wife reported sleeping soundly through the night while they were at the hotel. Perhaps Sarah was afraid the guests would be subjected to a draft if the window remained open overnight. The couple added that they felt comforted by what they perceived as the special presence in their room.

The price of accommodation at the Prince of Wales Hotel in Waterton National Park has certainly changed over the years but you can still count on attentive staff, luxurious amenities, glorious scenery and—as in the past fifty years—a ghost or two.

ROOM SIX RECEIVES
SPECIAL ROOM SERVICE

This Alberta ghost story travelled many kilometres to end up right back here where it belongs—in its home province. The following incident, which occurred in the mountain-park town of Banff, was reported to the century-old Institute for Psychical Research in London, England. The name of the hotel where the unexplained event took place has, unfortunately, been lost somewhere along the tale's trek. As the lodge is described as being "small, cozy and friendly" we can rule out the larger and more formal hotels in the town.

The story goes that a family named Fourche was touring western Canada. Fourteen-year-old Sonya Fourche had insulin-dependent diabetes and was well used to dealing with her body's special requirements. With a minimum of assistance, Sonya led a normal, happy and productive life.

As the family checked into hotels across the country they always arranged for an 8 AM wake-up call for Sonya. No matter how tired the girl was, she needed to be up at that time in order to eat a nourishing breakfast and inject her medication, because her health depended on conscientiously adhering to a strict schedule. The evening they arrived in Banff was no exception. As they checked into the hotel, weary from a full day's travel, Mr Fourche arranged for a wake-up call to be made to his daughter's room the next morning.

The next morning, precisely at 8 o'clock, the phone in room six rang. The clerk greeted Sonya with a cheery good morning and assured her that breakfast would be at her door in less than five minutes. The young woman barely had time to complete her early morning insulin routine before a delicious meal was delivered to her door. She ate her breakfast and waited for her parents, asleep in the next room, to awaken, and for the day's adventures to begin.

The Fourche family spent the day exploring all they could in Banff National Park. They returned to their hotel exhausted but pleased with the day. Before retiring to their respective rooms, Sonya and her father reminded the desk clerk of the importance of the next day's wake-up call.

When they were assured that the request had been duly recorded and would most certainly be followed up on, the father and daughter bid each other a good night and retired to their separate rooms.

Just as it had the first morning, the ringing of Sonya's phone awakened her the next morning, accompanied by a message virtually identical to the one the day before. Surprised at how tired she still felt, the youngster was able to make herself get out of bed only by remembering how good breakfast had been the day before and by anticipating a similar treat momentarily. She took care of her daily injection and then checked outside her door to see if breakfast had arrived yet. It hadn't, she was disappointed to note, so Sonya decided to get washed. She hurried in the shower so that her breakfast would still be hot when she brought it in from the hallway outside her door, but when she looked a second time, the meal still hadn't been delivered.

After checking a third and fourth time to see if room service had been there yet, Sonya gave up and went into her parents' bedroom to ask what they thought she should do about the tardy service. Much to her surprise, Sonya's parents were still fast asleep. She wakened her mother, who groggily asked what time it was. Sonya replied that it had to be 8:30 by now, because the phone call to waken her had come at least half an hour ago.

With that, both Sonya and Mrs Fourche glanced at the latter's travel alarm clock...and saw that it was not even 5 o'clock in the morning yet. The clock had to be wrong. The desk clerk wouldn't have made the call more than three hours too early. Sonya returned to her room, where she checked her wristwatch. Sure enough, the time shown by her watch matched what her mother's clock had read. Apparently someone had called Sonya's room and disturbed her sleep hours before she needed to be awake.

Thinking that a hotel employee had played a rather cruel practical joke, Mrs Fourche told Sonya that she would deal with the issue after a few more hours of sleep. She suggested her daughter also try to get back to sleep. Fortunately the girl's insulin dosage had been regulated successfully for a number of months and so, although the premature injection was not a good thing, it would not cause any harm.

As no one was able to fall back to sleep too soundly, Sonya and her parents were up and dressed just before 8 AM. They met in the hallway between their two rooms and decided to deal with the problem at the front desk before they went for breakfast.

Mr Fourche approached the clerk and reminded him of his obligation to phone Sonya's room. The clerk acknowledged the responsibility and apologized. He explained that he was running two or three minutes behind schedule in making the morning calls. Sonya replied that someone who was more than three hours ahead of schedule had already made the call.

The desk clerk stared uncomprehendingly before explaining that such an early morning call was an impossibility at that hotel. Not only was the front desk not staffed before 8 o'clock in the morning, but the bells on the telephones in the rooms were always turned off throughout the night so that the guests would not be disturbed.

For a few seconds, Mr Fourche and the desk clerk stared at one another over the counter. Neither was pleased with the way the conversation had gone. Just as Mr Fourche turned from the front desk in exasperation, the clerk called him back. He'd just remembered that he'd given Sonya room six—the haunted room. As best he could, the hotel employee explained that Sonya's experience was not the first incident in that particular room. Judging by similar events in the past, the teenager's early morning wake-up call had been initiated by an overly dedicated employee—one who had been dead for several years.

The clerk produced a notebook from under the counter. He asked the family to record the event alongside reports from others who'd stayed in room six. Annoyed and somewhat shaken, the Fourches refused the request and checked out of the hotel.

Apparently Mr Fourche waited until the family vacation was over before contacting the Institute for Psychical Research and telling them of their experience. The institute immediately contacted the hotel where the staff not only confirmed the family's story but eagerly shared the contents of the journal to which the Fourches had refused to contribute.

BANFF SPRINGS HOTEL UPDATE

In June 1995 I was invited to attend a reception at the Banff Springs Hotel, to celebrate the launching of an hour-long television special documenting some of the haunted places in western Canada. The party was held in a suite of rooms just off the elegant Rob Roy Dining Room.

This location hadn't been chosen at random: it was there that, over the years, many hotel employees had reported seeing an apparition of a bride dancing a solitary waltz. The image is widely believed to be the ghost of a bride who died there on her wedding day. She was making her entrance down a spiral staircase when the train of her bridal gown brushed up against the candles used to light the stairs. The young woman panicked and fell to the bottom of the stairs, where she died instantly, her neck broken.

Shortly after her death, the staircase was bricked up. The result was a stairway that went up about a dozen stairs before ending abruptly at a solid brick wall—a strange sight indeed. When I heard that work crews were tearing down the brick wall, I was curious as to whether this renovation might provoke some additional ghostly activity. Hoping to allow time for an encounter to occur, I let a couple of months go before calling the hotel with my inquiry.

The hotel's public relations department was delighted to report that the demolition had revealed a fabulous stone floor of which they hadn't been aware, but that was pretty much all. To date there had been no further sightings of the slightly transparent dancing bride.

To my knowledge, no one in our group of celebrants saw the long-deceased bride either, but the location of our gathering certainly did provoke some additional stories. A young woman serving at the party informed me that one particular elevator in the hotel will always return to the ninth floor. That's where Sam McCauley, a former bellboy at the hotel, was rumoured to have hidden his tips. McCauley is still seen helping out around the hotel occasionally—although he's been dead for nearly fifty years.

The ghost stories about the bride and the bellboy are well known, but the story Lethbridge resident Mike Prokop told me of an incident at the luxurious hotel was one I'd never heard before.

Mike and his friend Robert William were driving back home after a trip to the west coast. They had intended to make it as far as Calgary before stopping for the night, but bad weather forced them to cut short the day's drive at Banff.

"It was raining too hard to drive. It was late, about 11 PM, by the time we arrived in Banff. We tried all the hotels we could find but they were all booked so we went to 'the big hotel,'" he explained.

Considering that they were not looking for the luxurious accommodation that the Banff Springs Hotel provides, just overnight shelter from inclement weather Mike reported that they found the hotel a bit pricey.

"But we just couldn't make it to Calgary. We had something to eat and a beer and then went to our room. I have a habit when I'm staying in a hotel of leaving the bathroom light on and the bathroom door ajar so that if I wake up in the middle of the night I know where I am," Mike supplied.

The two weary travellers fell asleep almost immediately, the light from the bathroom casting a reassuring glow over them. In the middle of the night Mike was awakened by the sound of the toilet in their room flushing.

"Is that you, Bob?" he called out.

"No," his friend replied, "I'm right here. The maid went in there. I saw her go in."

As soon as the man heard himself say those words he knew that what he'd thought he'd seen couldn't possibly have happened. Both men jumped up and checked the door to their room. It was still as they'd left it when they retired, locked with the security chain in place. They were dumbfounded. Bob had been awake when he'd seen the image walk into the bathroom and both men had heard the toilet flush, but there was no one there—no one that they could see, anyway.

Neither man slept much after that. "We only stayed long enough to have a bit of breakfast the next morning and then we were on our way," my informant admitted.

To this day both men are convinced that their sleep on that rainy night was disturbed by a ghost who was totally unaware of their presence in "her" room.

THE CRONQUIST HOUSE

Red Deer's Cronquist House owes its continued existence to a group of hard-working concerned citizens. Unfortunately, one of their first acts in securing preservation annoyed the ghost in the in the huge home.

"The house has been moved," explained Elizabeth Plumtree, executive director of the society that now runs the house. "We think that's why he's mad."

"He" is presumed to be the ghost of Elias Cronquist, an elderly man when he died in the house in 1973. Elias had lived in the house virtually all his life. His parents had brought him and his three siblings to Alberta from their native Sweden in 1911, whereupon, according to Elizabeth Plumtree, they built this big splendid home.

Of the four Cronquist children, only one married. Another was killed in the war. Elias and one other sibling lived on in the family home.

"I understand he was quite eccentric by the end. He was alone in this huge four-storey house, but he only lived in one room. He died a bachelor," Elizabeth recounts.

There were no heirs to the estate and the house sat empty for years after the old man's death. In 1976, when the Alberta economy was booming, the land on which the Cronquist House sat was purchased by a developer. The company intended to cash in on the migration of families to the newly prosperous province by building a subdivision full of new housing. The developer had no use for the old run-down mansion that sat in the middle of its real estate acquisition and was going to demolish it just to get it out of the way.

At the same time, the Red Deer Cultural Heritage Society had just decided that it needed a place to establish headquarters. A deal was struck between the two disparate outfits. The developer was spared the expense of tearing the deteriorated place down by donating the house to the society, which in turn would acquire a much-needed home base.

Elizabeth Plumtree explained that the people of Red Deer rallied around the project with heartwarming enthusiasm. While the society raised funds to help support the mammoth project of moving the enormous house, other members of the community were also at work. People and companies donated time, expertise, labour and equipment to help make moving the Cronquist House, and preserving it, a reality.

Unfortunately, poor old Elias was apparently not a man who took to change easily—even today, more than twenty years after the fact, he's still objecting to the relocation.

"We'll come into the house in the morning and the doors will be swinging madly. The house is operated as a tea house now and occasionally table settings, cups and saucers will be totally moved. Doors will slam when there's no one near them," Elizabeth recounted calmly. She quite enjoys the presence, though. "It enhances the fabric of life, I think," she acknowledged.

When a new employee started work there recently, he was greeted with a loud crash. Elizabeth tried to reassure the startled man by crediting Elias with having made the racket. Others have reported that their backs become cold all over—a sure sign that a spirit is just behind you.

Next time you're in Red Deer, drop in at the Cronquist House and enjoy a light lunch. Don't worry if your table setting is moved around. That will just be Elias joining you for the meal.

GRANNY MACKAY'S PLACE

Jacqueline Chalmers knew she was taking on an enormous number of responsibilities when she began the work necessary to create a restaurant from a long-abandoned homestead near Millarville, south of Calgary. An unforeseen obligation, however, did take her completely by surprise. Jacqueline had no idea that she would be responsible for contributing to a long-deceased lady's sense of happiness and contentment.

"I always felt an energy in this place, that it needed laughter and life." Jacqueline continued, "Since [my family and I] have moved in here, the ghost must be happy. It's a very active home and aside from one instance when we first moved in there's been no more [ghostly] activity."

That certainly wasn't the case when Jacqueline first took over the old MacKay homestead and opened her pioneer-style restaurant. While the creation of the dining room imbued the place with some laughter and life, "it wasn't consistent energy," Jacqueline realizes now.

Vibrancy of any sort had been nonexistent at the MacKay family home for many years before Jacqueline bought it. Built in 1895, the house had been home to the MacKay family from 1916 until 1972, when Angus MacKay, the last of the descendants to live in the house, died. After his death, the home sat empty for nearly twenty years, until the entrepreneurial Jacqueline began reclaiming this one small piece of south-central Alberta's history.

Shortly after taking over, Jacqueline commented that the first tentative explorations into the house were like opening a time capsule. "It was like time stood still," she once told a reporter. She not only found clothes still hanging in closets, but even food in the cupboards.

To someone with different plans, this detritus might have been an inconvenience, but for Jacqueline every article she found was part of the area's heritage, a valuable artifact to be carefully restored and preserved. The only concessions she was willing to make to modern times were the kitchen and washroom facilities that she needed to add.

Not long after taking possession of the homestead, Jacqueline opened the restaurant, which she respectfully named, "The MacKay Place."

Word of the special "new" restaurant in the historic setting spread. People began making a special point to visit Millarville and to enjoy lunch in the ambiance Jacqueline had painstakingly recreated. Not all of her guests, however, left at closing time. There was evidence right from the start that someone else wanted to have a hand in running the new business.

"We had a clock on a windowsill in the kitchen. It was just a $10 clock. I won't say it was ugly but it certainly was bright and colourful," Jacqueline recalled. "One morning I came in and the clock was on the floor. At the time I didn't think anything of it. I just presumed it had fallen so I picked it up and put it back on the sill. The next morning it was on the floor again but this time both the hands were off the clock. I picked it up, fixed the hands and put it back on the windowsill. The next morning the clock was on the floor again and again both the hands were off but this time only one of the hands was lying on the floor."

To this day no one's ever found the other hand for the clock and Jacqueline now believes that the spirit in the home just didn't like that particular clock.

"I think she thought it was too contemporary for the older style of the home," Jacqueline said.

The broken clock proved to be just the first of the ghost's attention-getting stunts.

"I had a dozen silk roses in an old enamel coffee pot," Jacqueline recounted. "When I came in one day they were gone. I thought, 'Darn. They've been stolen.'"

This disappearance was puzzling because she was sure the bouquet had been there when she'd locked up the night before. Later, when she found six of the missing roses outside, Jackie was relieved. Her relief turned to further concern when she discovered five more roses in a cupboard. While it was reasonable to think that a would-be thief might have suddenly suffered a pang of conscience and dropped the flowers on the way out, there was no way that anyone would have had access to that cupboard. More puzzling still was the whereabouts of the last missing silk flower.

"I've looked everywhere," she acknowledged. "But I've never found the twelfth rose."

While the incidents with the clock and the roses were puzzling, they didn't really upset anyone. Those experiences were still to come. Jacqueline recalled a receiving a frantic phone call from her staff at closing time one evening. They were terrified, having heard a gruff voice in a stairway that they presumed was empty. When she rushed over to the restaurant and searched the entire premises, Jacqueline found nothing, though she couldn't help but notice a heavy, oppressive atmosphere about the place. The next morning that feeling was gone entirely.

"Another time we had dinner guests. One of the women was a clairvoyant. She left her chair to use the washroom, which is located down a narrow hall. As she walked, she felt a cold draft blow up her dress," Jacqueline remembered. The woman was so unnerved by the experience that she went directly back to her place at the table without ever using the washroom.

Jacqueline feels that an experience that she herself had shortly after the cold draft episode was related to it.

"I was working in my office. Because we added on to the back of the place, the window in that room no longer looks outside. It's now an interior window. I was alone and really concentrating on my work when I became aware of a dark figure passing the office window. I looked up but no one was there. I had locked myself in but still I checked around because I felt there was someone there. I think it was the same being [that caused the cold draft in the hallway]."

Guests enjoying a meal on what was at the time an outside verandah noticed a rhythmic creaking throughout much of their meal. Finally, tiring of the sound, the mother asked her little boy if he was turning the rungs on his chair with his feet. The child attested that he was not and the creaking continued. This time a long-time neighbour offered the probable explanation: Mrs MacKay used to like to spend the early part of her evenings rocking in her rocking chair on the verandah.

The haunted MacKay Place restaurant has since become not only a bed and breakfast but also the Chalmers' family home. Although the spirit "makes us aware," as Jacqueline acknowledges, this latest incarnation of her former home seems to please long deceased Mrs MacKay for the entire group now lives happily in harmony.

LETHBRIDGE COFFEE SHOP

Several years ago Al Antcil began an ambitious business endeavour in downtown Lethbridge—he opened a bookstore and adjoining coffee shop. Al did much of the work to prepare the space for its new purposes himself. Considering the building was constructed in the very early days of the century, this preparation was quite an undertaking. It was during these renovations that he had his first encounter with the resident phantom.

"One day I was working in the basement, anchoring a half-wall," he recalled. "All of a sudden I got the creeps. I mean really got the willies. I got really scared. I thought to myself, "This is too weird. I'm shutting the place up and going home.""

Because these decidedly uncomfortable feelings had come on so suddenly, with no identifiable provocation, Al tried his best to put the entire experience out of his mind and get on with opening his business. To a great extent he was successful, until early one morning when he was baking cinnamon buns.

"I was working away when all of a sudden all the baking pans that we kept on top of the double-door refrigerator came flying off. They didn't just drop," he assured me, "They flew about ten feet. I was too scared."

It was late at night, however, when Al was working in the bookstore that he had his biggest fright.

"It was about 2 AM and I was doing the store accounts. Suddenly I heard 'Bump, bump, bump, bump.' I went out from the office and saw that some books had fallen. I didn't think much of it—books fall, I just picked them up and went back to what I was doing. Then I heard 'Bump, bump, bump, bump, bump, bump.' This time about twenty books had fallen. I thought maybe a bus had gone past and the rumble had knocked the books off. I put them back up and again went back to my work."

Al Antcil wasn't quite as calm with the next series of bumps. He ran into the store to find every book had fallen from its shelf and now lay on the floor. For the second time since he had opened his adjoining businesses, the man beat a hasty retreat to the security of his home.

About two years later, one of Al's employees actually saw the apparition. According to Al, "Grant Smith was a great big guy, about 6 feet 1 inch and 280 pounds. He played football for the Hamilton Tiger Cats. One day he walked out from the back and the way he swung his head around I knew he'd seen something. He turned white. I asked him what was wrong and he said he'd seen a woman, but she's not there now."

Al was actually somewhat relieved by the sighting. "At least we know it's a woman," he commented at the time. Oddly, that sighting marked the last of the ghostly high jinks, although Al readily admits that "no one ever works here alone and no one will go into the basement, except me. I still don't like it down there but I know I have to go there sometimes. I've actually spoken out loud to the presence when I've been downstairs."

Al has tried to probe into the haunting by questioning fellow business owners on the block. He can't get much confirmed but has heard rumours that a nearby building once housed a brothel and that the ghost may be the former madam. He also heard that nearby businesses have had similar problems.

"Apparently they were hearing voices. They got a Christian counsellor or minister to deal with it," he reported.

Since those first ambitious days of owning both the adjoining retail outlets, Al has sold B. Macabee's Bookstore to Leona King, who has quite a different take on why the ghost quieted down so suddenly.

"I hired Keith McArthur as assistant manager. There haven't been any occurrences since then," she reported happily.

Keith, a self-professed skeptic, replied to the implication that his presence might have put an end to the haunting by stating that "everyone else talks about ghosts. I talk about gravity."

Whatever the origin, whatever the remedy, the bottom line remains the same for these businesses. They're no longer bothered by their once-resident spirit.

THE GHOSTS OF JASPER PARK LODGE

People from all over the world come to Alberta to stay at the Jasper Park Lodge. And it's no wonder—the lodge really does have it all, including luxurious surroundings and an alert, capable staff to cater to your every need. All of this, nestled in the grandeur of the Canadian Rockies. Oh yes, and ghosts too.

Mario Rulli, sales co-ordinator for the establishment, explained that most of the haunting at the lodge seems to be done by a former employee believed to haunt the Point Cabin.

"Supposedly, in the late '40s or early '50s, a chambermaid was climbing the stairs [in the Point Cabin] that lead to a small card room. A guest surprised her...and she fell backwards, tumbling down the stairs and breaking her neck, causing her death," Mario related. "Since that incident, there have been numerous happenings in the Point Cabin."

One of those happenings occurred during the winter in an era when the hotel was open only during the summer months.

"There were workers in the cabin doing slight renovations [to] the interior. This involved placing the furniture in the middle of the room. Every morning when they came back to the cabin...they found the furniture had been moved all about," he began. "A couple of them decided to investigate, anticipating that it was staff fooling around. As they approached the cabin they noticed the lights were on, but when they entered, the lights were off. No one was in the cabin. They exited the cabin and decided to hide a few feet away so they could catch the prankster. They saw lights turn on and smoke coming out of the chimney."

Showing a remarkable amount of courage, the pair ran inside the cabin again. They found a dark room with no fire in the fireplace. Worse, the furniture had been rearranged. They looked around for footprints in the snow surrounding the cabin but found none.

The employees couldn't have been entirely surprised by the situation, because the haunting of the Point Cabin is well known around the lodge. The switchboard has received calls from the cabin, and people have reported seeing lights going on and off—all when the cabin was unoccupied. When the cabin is occupied, the television has been known to develop a mind of its own and change channels by itself.

But the maid in the Point Cabin isn't the only ghost at Jasper Park Lodge. There are also the dining-room ghosts. Apparently these two are an elderly couple who suddenly appear and then just as suddenly disappear from the hotel's dining room.

"The ghosts seem harmless but enjoy watching staff run hysterically out of [the] room," according to Mario Rulli.

Considering the advantages you enjoy when staying at Jasper Park Lodge, it shouldn't be too much of a surprise that at least a few souls have chosen to make this luxurious hotel their very permanent home.

CHAPTER 5

EERILY ENTERTAINING

THE EMPRESS THEATRE

The Empress Theatre in Fort Macleod is the oldest functioning theatre in western Canada. It has a proud and colourful past. It also has a ghost.

Construction of the theatre began in 1910. This milestone was noted this way in the January 20th edition of the *Lethbridge Daily Herald*: "Macleod is to have a new opera house. In every particular, except size, it will not be surpassed by any in the province. There will be...every modern accessory of a first-class theatre. It will be...a great addition to the appearance of the town's chief thoroughfare."

Two years later, Main Street's new crown jewel was completed. At its opening, the Empress became the fourth theatre in the little town of Macleod. Over time, the other three playhouses have become history, leaving the Empress as Fort Macleod's only theatre. The historical society responsible for maintaining the place today explains, "The Empress Theatre has always played an important role in the community." It has served as a vaudeville house, a concert hall and a lecture hall; as well as having served as a venue for live entertainment, in its most recent incarnation it has become a movie house.

Given the cast of characters that have entertained their way across the Empress's stage, it's not surprising that there have been a few psychic imprints left behind. After all, what self-respecting Albertan in 1935 would have thought of missing a performance by "Texas Tony and his Wonder Horse Baby Doll, accompanied by the Purple Sage Riders"? Surely folks must have traveled from far around to witness such an entertainment event! More recently, the place hosted a sold-out crowd after booking Sarah McLachlin for a performance.

Both of those performers and many others left their comments on the downstairs graffiti wall. Some members of Sarah McLachlin's crew also left with stories to tell their grandchildren. Two of the roadies were standing on stage after a performance when they heard footsteps go by them. Later, when their work was done and they were relaxing over a celebratory bottle of beer, they heard scratching noises at the door. Despite their careful investigations, no source was ever found for the sounds. These two normally pragmatic "meat and potatoes guys" also watched a blind in the theatre being snapped back and forth when there was no one near it.

A few years ago, the ghost at the Empress Theatre managed to pull off an expensive prank. He was apparently responsible for a banging sound emanating from the hot-water pipes. Because the theatre's administrators had no idea the sounds were being mystically produced, they went to all the trouble and expense of having the offending pipes removed. Unfortunately, even though it was now physically impossible, the sound of pipes banging persisted.

Some parts of the auditorium are more haunted than others. Actor Bruce Watson described feeling "a cold spot at the front of the house." He also reported that, "Last summer I had a strange feeling someone was standing over my left shoulder down the back stage staircase. I mean, I really felt like there was someone there."

The man's report is in keeping with other accounts, for it is in the same spot that many people report feeling a presence and where an actor reported seeing an apparition while he was on stage. In another sighting, a former employee saw the ghost too. In both cases the viewer described a man "with big, hairy arms, wearing a brown shirt."

Although he didn't have time to note the entity's appearance, Mike Ford, an employee of the society that operates the theatre, remembers not only the time the ghost ran past him but also hearing the phantom when he thought he was alone in the concession booth.

A little girl once had an experience that she's not likely to ever forget. She went into the basement washroom and, while standing at the sink, glanced up at the mirror. There, staring at her, was a man's face hanging suspended a little above her eye level. When the child whirled around to confront the intruder, she saw that she was, in fact, alone in the washroom. Being the solitary occupant didn't console her enough to allow for lingering. The child ran to her mother, who then reported the incident to the theatre's staff. There was little they could do except to chalk up another sighting of their ghost. All the sightings have resulted in amazingly similar descriptions of the apparition.

The Empress Theatre

There is great debate as to who the ghost might be. Some think it's the spirit of long-time owner and manager Dan Boyle, who bought the place in 1937. Others, like Diana Segboer of the Empress Theatre Society, think the ghost is Ed, a former caretaker. Either assumption is reasonable.

Dan owned the theatre for many years. He was responsible for many of the functional and decorative upgrades that grace the theatre today. With Dan Boyle having devoted so much of his life to the place, it wouldn't be surprising to think that he decided to oversee the theatre into eternity.

Ed, the former maintenance man, is an equally convincing candidate. So convincing, in fact, that Empress employee Bonnie Himsl readily admits she greets the ghost with a cheery, "Hi, Ed," as she enters the place every morning.

Ed was apparently very devoted to his job but he was also devoted to his considerably more profitable sideline—bootlegging. It was that part-time occupation that eventually led to Ed's demise. He was found murdered, his body unceremoniously left on the grounds of the Auction Market. No one was ever brought to justice for the lethal act. Because the ghost's presence in the Empress is often accompanied by phantom smells of liquor and tobacco, Diana thinks it's Ed's spirit.

Whoever he is, Dan or Ed, the ghost at the Empress is certainly emotionally attached to the place. During a particularly unsettling time in the theatre's recent history, staff members heard crying coming from somewhere in the empty building. "[The ghost] seems to pick up on bad vibrations," they agreed.

And he certainly doesn't want to be forgotten.

As Diana explained, "I've heard him walking in the theatre and the alarm goes off lots. He's also tapped on the projection booth window."

Another employee was pushed down some stairs by the force of an invisible hand between her shoulder blades. That incident was unusual, for most frequently the spectre seems to want to stay out of the way. When people are upstairs, they generally hear him going about his ghostly affairs downstairs. When people are downstairs, he's often heard on the balcony.

One day as Diana entered the building accompanied by another woman, she called out a greeting to the presence and then the two women went about their business. "Joyce was humming a tune," she recalled. "When she stopped, Ed whistled its ending."

Some of the spirit's pranks can be quite unnerving to theatre staff as they try to clean up after a performance. They know the ghost is about because they can hear him walking. But that's not the worst of it. "Sometimes when you're sweeping up, you can pick up the same wrapper four times," explains one staff member.

The seats in the theatre are spring loaded to fold up out of the way when they are not occupied. Sometimes Ed or Dan will put on quite a show for the people closing up. They watch in amazement as the seats go up and down seemingly of their own accord.

The spirit is not a shy one. While he has often been active when the theatre is full, on these occasions he has usually preferred to communicate with someone who was alone in a room. Despite this apparent preference, the entity has occasionally shown off to a group of people. A group gathered around drinking coffee watched in collective amazement as a coffee cup moved around a table, seemingly of its own accord. Thinking that either the bottom of the cup or the surface of the table was wet, someone picked it up to wipe any such friction-reducing moisture away. The tactic might actually have worked, except that both the cup and the table were dry. When put back down, the cup moved again.

During some recent renovations there was a layer of sawdust on the floor. A group of people clearly heard footsteps but did not see anyone nor were there any footprints left behind in the sawdust.

Occasionally too, something at the Empress will prohibit the employees from opening the safe. The combination that worked well the day before will, every so often, just not open the vault. The last time the locking mechanism was thrown out of kilter Bonnie Himsl lost her patience and "really told [the ghost] off." Since then there hasn't been a problem.

Perhaps the spirit realized that that particular action was especially annoying to the present-day staff. He may crave attention, but like most of us, he doesn't enjoy being in trouble.

Former Empress Theatre employee Trent Moroz noted that the feeling of the presence had been "especially strong after [showing certain] films." He said that sometimes when he was locking up he could "feel a cold breath from the theatre itself." Only a thoroughly haunted building could evoke such a description.

Perhaps future job ads should include a caution discouraging easily spooked potential employees.

"WE DO HAVE A GHOST AT THE PRINCESS"

Theatres are often given regal names: the Royal, the Empress and the Princess are common monikers. During certain later periods of a theatre's lifetime, these pretentious names can be in stunning contradiction to their states of disrepair.

For a time, this situation was certainly the case with Edmonton's Princess Theatre. When it opened in 1915, the Princess was proclaimed as one of the grandest houses, boasting "the largest stage in Western Canada and promis[ing] a program of high class moving pictures varied occasionally with high class musical vaudeville or musical concerts." Until 1940, the Princess reigned alone in its splendour as the only theatre on Edmonton's south side. By the time it was closed in 1958, the place was badly run down, with only its name remaining grand.

During the next fifteen years, the theatre deteriorated even further as parts of the building were used intermittently as retail outlets and other areas remained vacant—or more correctly, almost vacant.

During the theatre's design in 1914, architects Wilson and Herrald incorporated a couple of unusual and potentially profitable additions into their plans. For instance, the building's basement became home to a billiards club and, though the cinema with its balcony and projection booth took up two full storeys, above the auditorium Mr Wilson and Mr Herrald included an additional level. This floor was rented out over the years, first as office space and later as a rooming house.

The Princess didn't welcome another theatre audience until 1973.

While the theatre's reopening was decidedly low key, it attracted sufficient attention to lead to government recognition of the facility as a historical resource. Today it has been restored and is operated by the Old Strathcona Foundation as Edmonton's only repertory theatre. Its location for this purpose couldn't be better. Nestled among the shops, restaurants and coffee houses of the once-again-popular Whyte Avenue the Princess is a favourite with film buffs of all ages and inclinations. It's also haunted.

Staff at the Princess speak openly about their experiences with the ghost, their only regret being that they're not sure who the ghost could be or if there's only one. Former director Brian Paisley is inclined to think the spirit is that of a previous tenant from the days when the third floor area was used as a rooming house. He knows he's heard the sound of footsteps coming from the storey above the theatre, which hasn't been occupied for years.

Mary Pearson, the theatre's manager, had a more direct experience with the ghost. "I was alone in the theatre. I had to go into the projection booth," she began, pausing in her story to explain that this part of the theatre juts out above the second-storey balcony seats. On this particular day, Mary was not to accomplish what she'd gone into the projectionist's area to do. Just as she began the task at hand, she heard knocking at the window.

It was a distinct sound. There was no mistaking it for anything else. Someone had knocked on the outside of the projection booth's front glass wall. Mary knew positively that she was alone, locked in an otherwise empty building. Although the experience frightened the young woman, it didn't surprise her completely, for she'd heard stories of the Princess's ghost from her colleagues. Mary knew she'd now experienced him too, because even if there'd been a full house, no ordinary human could have rapped on that window: for anyone (or anything) to have knocked on the glass, he or she would have had to have defied a basic law of nature by standing in mid-air. Badly shaken, Mary fled the building.

At least now Mary didn't need to feel left out when her co-workers told their tales about the ghost. By comparing experiences, employees at the Princess Theatre have come to the conclusion that, aside from his shock value, there is nothing innately frightening about their resident ghost. He apparently doesn't want to harm anyone, but he just doesn't seem to want to be forgotten either.

Leslea Kroll worked at the theatre from the summer of 1989 until the fall of 1992, managing it for the last year and a half of her tenure. As theatre manager, Leslea was required to begin work earlier than most of the other employees and so she was often alone in the cavernous old building.

"The first time I became aware of the ghost I was standing in the concession booth counting chocolate bars. I heard a knocking on the wall across the lobby," Leslea stated. "At that time there was a restaurant next door which closed early on Sundays. The restaurant was empty when I heard the sound."

Leslea found her own reaction to the experience as interesting as the experience itself. She's since noted that she has usually had a similar reaction to something that startled or concerned her: "I denied it. I thought, "No, I didn't hear that."

Unfortunately for Leslea Kroll's composure, the ghost didn't accept her denial reflex. "I heard it again. This time I said 'Hello,' and then it stopped."

Not wanting to risk losing her co-workers' respect, Leslea kept the experience to herself. Perhaps this limited reaction frustrated the ghost, because it tried again and again to get her attention. Finally she was forced into the comfort of sharing her ghostly secret. Again alone in the theatre, Leslea was on the phone, speaking with a friend. Perhaps upset that the young woman was paying attention to someone other than itself, the ghost knocked quite loudly. "My friend heard it [too]," explained a relieved but puzzled Leslea.

This incident began an exchange of ghostly experiences among Princess staff members. Most had at least occasionally been aware of a presence. For the woman who did the cleaning, who usually worked alone in the place, the ghostly knocking and footsteps had become regular, if unwelcome, additions to her working conditions.

By the autumn of 1992, for reasons not related to the ghost, Leslea decided to seek employment elsewhere. "On my second last day at the Princess I took someone up to the marquee room. We both heard the distinct sounds of footsteps on the stairs with us, although we saw no one and to our knowledge we were alone in a locked building."

Perhaps the ghost was coming up to say good-bye to his long-time friend, or perhaps he was finally feeling comfortable enough with Leslea that he would have begun to communicate with her more directly. We'll never know. We do know, however, that whoever or whatever haunts the Princess did not leave when Leslea did. The pragmatic Brian Paisley, attested to the continuing presence of the spirit with classic simplicity: "We do have a ghost here at the Princess."

CALGARY'S HAUNTED PLANETARIUM

It's always gratifying to watch the phone lines light up (and occasionally even jam!) when ghosts are the topic on television or radio phone-in shows. Interest in the subject of phantoms is clearly high. Many people have questions, but others have had experiences that they wish to share.

A gentleman who called John Hanlon's CBC radio show, *Wildrose Country*, told a marvellous tale about a ghost in Calgary's Centennial Planetarium (now the Calgary Science Centre). He had worked there as a volunteer when the building first opened in 1967. He described overseeing the audience settling in for a show in the star theatre. Most nights the process would be unremarkable, but every now and again someone would complain that there was a man who wouldn't sit down. When the staff went to check, the offending image would simply vanish.

This story was so enticing that I decided to visit the planetarium and see if I could get any more information.

"What your caller described was actually fairly common," acknowledged Marnie Heaney, house supervisor at the planetarium. "He's gone now, but he used to live in the old star theatre. We called him Sam. People would see him walking through the theatre [during the show] when all the doors were closed. Then he'd just disappear."

He certainly didn't leave the theatre by a conventional route, because opening any of the doors to the darkened theatre would have let a noticeable amount of light in. The apparition simply vanished, either into thin air or by walking through a wall. After a few incidents like this one, the staff at the planetarium came to realize that the man people occasionally saw walking around the theatre was not a flesh and blood human being but a phantom.

They began to pay more attention to the patrons' descriptions of the apparent intruder. "He looked like a World War I soldier," Marnie Heaney explained. "I've seen him quite often. He was an interesting guy. You'd see him walking across the theatre but I've also heard his footsteps in the main foyer. He'd follow you."

Marnie wonders if her strong Irish background could have made her more accepting of the phantom than other people might be. But even she had her uncomfortable moments.

"If I was alone in the building working late at night and I heard him I'd talk to him, tell him 'That's enough.' Normally he'd leave then," she recalled.

Like most ghosts, Sam wasn't a constant presence. He came and went, apparently on his own schedule. However, according to Marnie, "You'd know if he was around."

One day as Marnie and another employee worked, they could smell aftershave lotion. "We searched the building carefully and there was no one else here. The aftershave lotion smell was strongest in one particular spot and that spot was cold, very cold. After a while the smell just disappeared."

Other employees weren't quite as accepting of their ethereal co-worker as Marnie always was. "We've had cleaners refuse to go into the theatre. And one woman quit after she'd been sitting alone in the theatre and the seat beside her folded down, as though someone had just sat down in it," Marnie related.

During one period the experience of seeing Sam was dreaded by all on staff. "For a while it seemed that after every sighting something terrible would happen. A girl who worked here saw him and right after that her father died. Then a man had a stroke almost immediately after seeing Sam," Marnie recalled.

Thankfully, that pattern didn't continue. Working in a haunted place is one thing but to feel potentially jinxed by the ghost would not have improved employee morale.

"The staff got used to him," Marnie told me with a somewhat wistful tone in her voice.

"You sound as though you miss Sam," I probed.

"You know, I do miss him," Marnie replied with evident sincerity.

It's been years now since anyone's seen Sam. Today if the ghost in the World War I soldier's uniform came back to visit his old haunt, the star theatre, he'd hardly recognize the place. It's been completely renovated to take advantage of the incredible technological advances that have been made since the planetarium opened back in Canada's centennial year. The new theatre is certainly most impressive but it's not haunted, for now. Given the great attraction that spirits seem to feel to things electrical and electronic, the planetarium is most assuredly a likely future haunt.

Almost as if to bear out this theory, Marnie added in passing that "sometimes when you're downstairs in the lower area, you can hear a baby crying. A few people have heard it." Of course there were no babies anywhere around.

Perhaps one day the mystery of the phantom cries may be solved, but for now it only makes working at Calgary's Centennial Planetarium all the more interesting.

THE GHOST
OF SPEEDWAY PARK

Jerry Knowles was involved with Speedway Park Race Track, in northwestern Edmonton, from its inception in 1966 right through to the park's last car race in 1983. During those eighteen seasons he saw a tremendous number of changes at the track. He even saw the track, formerly a farmer's field, become haunted.

"There was a period of a few years [during which] quite a bit happened. We'd hear doors opening and closing in the tower when there was no one else around," he remembered.

The tower, the main building at the track, housed offices, a lounge and a press room. "The upper area had a wooden floor and you could hear someone walking on the floor above your head," Jerry commented, adding that these sounds occurred although the upper storey was empty at the time.

The incidents became so frequent that everyone around Speedway began to take the haunting for granted. "We always thought there was a friendly ghost there," he explained.

The spirit didn't haunt only the tower, however. It roamed throughout the park and could occasionally be heard on a set of metal steps at the side of the track. Once the ghost was actually even seen.

"We came out of the tower and there was a figure sitting in the stands. You could see it sitting in the top corner of the stands. Graham Light [an executive with the racing association] and I both saw it for about twenty seconds and then it was gone. We couldn't make out who it was," Jerry stated.

Jerry does, however, have his suspicions about who the ghost at the track could have been. "There was a young guy living in the basement of the tower. He was only about nineteen or twenty years old, a really friendly, nice young fellow and an unbelievable artist," Jerry described. "One summer he drove his car out just west of the city and he killed himself."

The sighting in the bleachers, the phantom footsteps and the sounds of doors slamming in the tower began after that young man's death. During our telephone interview Jerry and I debated briefly where the young man's spirit may have gone when the park was sold. As the young man loved car racing, I suggested that he may have followed his friends to their new premises in the Calmar area.

"Oh, no," Jerry stated simply. "The new track's not haunted at all."

Perhaps then, one of the houses in the subdivision where Speedway Park once stood is home to a ghost. Or perhaps the young man, who stayed on at the track even in death, has now gone to his final rest.

There is one other ghost story associated with Speedway Park Race Track. It predates the story of the young man's spirit and by now has become more like a legend. No one seems to know about the sighting first hand, only through other people's stories. It is clearly not the same apparition because this phantom is female. Her image used to be seen walking calmly about the track area. When a concerned race car enthusiast would approach her to offer assistance she would simply vanish.

Given that the land the track was laid out on used to be a farmer's field the apparition may have been the farm wife checking on her crops.

OSCAR, THE BAD-TEMPERED GHOST

There are many theories about what a ghost might be. One idea is that what we identify as a ghost is leftover energy. This theory is useful in explaining why places where traumas have occurred tend to be haunted. It also could explain why poltergeists are especially attracted to adolescents, whose developing bodies are highly energized by surging hormones. At a more mundane level, we often see that spirits are intrigued by electrical energy and can draw attention to themselves by turning appliances such as washing machines, televisions and VCRs on and off. Imagine, then, what fun a ghost would have surrounded by the electrical devices and energy at a radio station.

For many years CHCL, an all-volunteer organization, was the radio station at the Canadian Forces Base in Medley, Alberta. Former music director Graham Wood shared the story of the haunted station with folklore collector Kathryn Carter, who in turn, passed it along to me.

Wood explained early on in the report that he promised his fellow broadcasters they'd be guaranteed complete anonymity. For that reason, no names have been used throughout this chapter.

He began his story on a note that any ghost-hunter will find familiar. "There's a definite feeling of unease permeating the rooms at the station. It's a feeling of not quite being alone even though the rational part of us says that you're the only visible, flesh and blood creature present."

Many volunteer announcers at CHCL have questioned the wisdom of staying behind to do the late night show or getting up early to do the *Early Bird Show*. Being alone at the station, it seems, is just plain not comfortable.

No one at CHCL can remember who first began talking about Oscar. The legend was so widely accepted that veteran broadcasters wondered only when each new staff member would meet the resident phantom.

186 More Ghost Stories of Alberta

"Oscar is not a playful ghost, or at least his antics don't seem to be geared to entertain," Wood began. "To be fair, unless you count wear and tear on your nerves, Oscar doesn't seem to actively try to harm station members either. Oscar simply travels the halls, being his own ghostly self, and unless provoked, is rarely obviously present."

Research into who the ghost may have been when he was alive points to a lonely young serviceman.

"[He] departed this world rather suddenly one night over the Christmas holidays, back in the days when the rooms now housing CHCL were used as a barracks," Wood relayed. "It seems that Oscar, in his human form, had a habit of consuming copious amounts of alcohol and that this trait has followed him into the afterlife. In fact, one of the first signs that Oscar is back to haunt the living is the heavy smell of stale alcohol in the 45 [rpm records] library."

Like many folks who overindulge, Oscar occasionally found it difficult to control his emotions. Wood readily admitted he'd never stayed behind to witness these outbursts.

"But I have heard blow-by-blow accounts of Oscar's temper tantrums from people who were actually brave enough to stay at the station—even for a few moments—while Oscar was active. I don't believe anyone has remained for the whole show or at least if anyone has, they aren't talking. Usually these people decide that their curiosity has been satisfied at just about the time the plaques on the walls down the hallway begin to tremble [and then] the heating and water pipes begin to bang and the doorknobs begin to rattle from the pressure of unseen hands. You might say that these events are enough to encourage everyone to leave the station so that Oscar can finish his business in privacy."

A married couple who volunteered for the early shift one Saturday morning first became aware of Oscar's presence when they were in one of his favourite haunts, the 45 library. As they opened the door to that room, their nostrils were assaulted by odour of stale booze. As they were assessing the smell, a bone-chilling rush of frigid air rushed past them. Hoping the wind had come from an open window, the couple made their way across the room, prepared to close the offending window.

"Their skeptical attitude changed quickly as they discovered the window to be tightly closed and felt the comforting heat of the radiator," Wood reported. "They...concluded that there was no immediate need to pull the records for their early morning show, and rapidly departed for the more comfortable atmosphere of the library where the long-playing records are stored. They closed the door to the 45 library as they left."

Cold spots, or the absence of heat, are common characteristics of a haunted area. It is often presumed that the spirit draws the heat energy right out of the air. This certainly seemed to be the case at the Armed Forces radio station in Medley. According to Graham Wood, staff apparently found a practical solution to dealing with these chilled areas. "Most people have learned to simply avoid these pockets while going about their business. Sooner or later Oscar will move on and the cold spot will warm up again."

Oscar's musical preferences apparently did not die with him. "There are songs at the station that some people absolutely refuse to play after Oscar has very noisily expressed his opinion of them."

He will also, on occasion, play his own music. "Various DJs have reported that every now and then music can be heard playing in rooms other than the regular studio. Upon investigation, [they] discover that all of the rooms are vacant and they can only conclude that Oscar's busy again expressing his individuality by playing his own choice of music instead of listening to the fare provided by the on-air DJ."

We often associate ghosts with darkened areas but Wood reports that Oscar likes the lights on. "One conscientious announcer did the station shut-down late one night. He diligently turned off lights, emptied trash cans and locked all the doors. When he arrived downstairs and walked across the parking lot to his car he glanced up at the second floor to do a final visual check only to see all the lights blazing again. The man may have been conscientious but he wasn't stupid. He decided if Oscar wanted a dozen night lights he should have them."

Graham Wood concluded his story with an invitation to any doubters to stay alone in the CHCL building. Unfortunately, that test is no longer available, as the radio station ceased operation a few years ago.

"POLTIE" DID IT

It is a well-documented fact that several people watching the same event will report the occurrence very differently. People who have stood together and watched a person commit a crime will give totally different descriptions of the criminal. Surprisingly, this ghost story contradicts that peculiarity of human nature, which makes the tale even more intriguing. The story of the haunting has been told to me four different times by four very different people, one of whom lives more than a thousand kilometres away, and yet it is the similarities in their stories, rather than the differences, that are notable.

The story in question revolves around a radio station in Edmonton. Despite the well-accepted existence of the station's ghost, management's official stance is to deny any knowledge of such a phenomenon and so, sadly, the station will not be identified in this story, and any personal names used are fictitious.

A radio station haunting isn't too surprising considering that visiting spirits are often attracted to sources of electrical or electronic energy. Given this taste for electricity, a venue emitting one hundred thousand watts of power must provide a spiritual smorgasbord for a ghost.

Stories of this haunting date back nearly fifteen years and continue to this day. When one former employee of the station began work there in the early 1980s, she found people had a ready excuse for everything from malfunctioning equipment to missing office supplies. "Poltie did it," she was told. Although she never had a personal experience with the ghost, she made a point of collecting first-hand accounts from colleagues who had.

For those of us not familiar with the inner workings of a radio station, my informant explained how "it's not unusual to see unfamiliar faces around any station. There are always people coming and going."

Still, employees always knew when the stranger in the hall was the ghost and not merely an unfamiliar advertising client. The ghost appeared only either very late in the evening or in the wee hours of the morning. Their second—and no doubt more convincing—clue about the visitor's identity was that, although the ghost was easily visible, closer assessment revealed that he existed only him from the knees up.

The ghost is that of a young man, possibly of native Canadian descent. He wears a dark bomber-style jacket of denim or leather. His appearances at the station inevitably coincide with a near epidemic of irritatingly misplaced items. Pens, log books and tape cartridges would go missing from the control room, only to show up exactly where they had been left and searched for in the first place.

While the spirit's favourite spot was clearly the control room, he also enjoyed visiting the news room, the music library and the announcers' lounge. Staff members routinely reported walking through cold spots in these rooms, and occasionally even declared that they had seen the apparition. An announcer who left the lounge for a few minutes returned to see his coffee cup, still full of steaming brew, sitting suspended in mid-air. The cup stayed there, defying all natural laws, until the man reached out to grasp it. Then it fell to the floor.

One of the station's writers, who was experiencing some difficulties in his personal life, often spent his off hours at work visiting with the announcers. One particular night he was perched on a stool, close to the console, when a sudden force sent him flying off backward, up against the wall. This clearly malevolent display was enough to make the staff members who had seen the ghost join forces and take action.

One of the newscasters had a friend with psychic talents in Ontario. Late one evening, the half-dozen people who had seen or felt Poltie met in the largest studio and used the speaker-phone to make a prearranged call to the out-of-province sensitive. Following introductions and a thorough explanation of the situation, the psychic made a few comments, beginning with the theory of a spirit's attraction to electricity.

Then, to everyone's amazement, he accurately described the entity they had all been seeing. Later, when the psychic spoke privately to his friend from the news room, he revealed that describing the apparition had been a simple matter, as he had been mentally tuned to the people on the other end of the phone—and the ghost had been right there with them.

More disturbing still was the psychic's description of the violent incident involving the writer being thrown off the stool. The attack, the psychic determined, had been an attempted possession. Apparently, the writer's personal problems had made him weak and therefore vulnerable to such an attack.

As any friend would, the man reported these details to the troubled writer, whose response was swift and sure. The writer left the very next day on an unplanned but much needed vacation.

Another instance occurred when an off-duty announcer returned to the station to put away the equipment he'd had with him while supplying the music at a local dance.

It was 2 or 3 o'clock in the morning, one of Poltie's favourite times. Dave was carrying equipment down a hallway, past the music director's office. The lights in the office were turned off, as he'd expected they would be, but from behind the closed door he could clearly hear desk drawers being opened and closed.

Understandably unnerved, he reported this odd state of affairs to Tony in the control room. As he spoke, a gust of extremely cold wind blew through the control room, which had neither a door nor a window open. Seconds later, like the writer before him, Dave was thrown from his chair and hurled against a wall. The terrified pair retreated to Dave's truck and returned to the building only when records needed to be changed.

After a few trips in and out, the men began to feel a little foolish and, deciding the incidents must all have a rational explanation, returned to the building. They checked the music director's office first to see why Dave had heard desk drawers being slammed. Nothing in the small room seemed out of place—until a coffee cup rose from the desk, sat suspended for a minute in mid-air, then travelled over to where they stood and dropped on the carpet at their feet.

Suddenly the pair once again saw the wisdom of their decision to sit in the truck between record changes. Unfortunately, the spirit's strength was increasing with each antic. This time, as soon as they reentered the building, all the power went out.

Now they really had to do something. A radio station that isn't broadcasting isn't accomplishing anything for anyone. They called the station's engineer and waited, outside, for him to arrive. Perhaps Dave and Tony had intended to explain the night's goings-on to the engineer, but he arrived still groggy from his disturbed sleep and not in very good humour. That less-than-positive mood did not improve when the engineer located the source of the problem: the main breaker switch on the electrical panel had been moved to the off position. He flipped the switch back to the on position where it belonged and, of course, once again everything in the station worked as it should have.

By this time the early morning staff had begun to arrive. Jeff, the disk jockey, and Paula, the newscaster, set about their familiar routine in separate rooms adjoined by a plate-glass window. Just before the first news broadcast, Paula watched Jeff whirl around in his chair and stare at the door to his announcing booth.

"There's somebody in here," he exclaimed. "While you do the news I'm going to look around."

Jeff was back moments later and reported that he hadn't found anything out of the ordinary. This surprised him, he said, because he'd felt someone staring at him and when he turned to identify the source of the creepy feeling he'd seen a very tall figure in what looked like a bomber-style jacket.

The on-air duo were uncharacteristically jumpy for the balance of their shift and they felt cold breezes brushing by every once in a while, even though they remained in separate, closed-off rooms. They were both relieved when they saw their counterparts for the next show arrive. Jeff told the other announcer that "something weird is going on" but didn't mention the cold air or seeing the image.

"Funny you should mention that," the second announcer replied. "I had a strange experience here just last week."

He then proceeded to describe seeing the figure that Jeff had noticed. Word then spread and a badly shaken staff met on Monday morning to compare stories. Many people had seen the same image but, fearing for their jobs, no one had shared the information with others. Apparently Poltie had even made himself known to at least one non-employee. A disk jockey explained that his girlfriend, who frequently used to visit him at work, will no longer come near the place.

"She was sitting in the music director's office one day waiting for me to finish. The zipper on her purse opened and then closed again, on its own, as she stared in horrified amazement."

Not everyone was that susceptible. An announcer, obviously devoid of any love of mystery, unwrapped a brand new reel-to-reel audio tape. It should, of course, have been blank but when the man wound it up on the machine and pressed "play" to advance it a little, the tape emitted strange, garbled noises. Curious, he changed the speed of the tape but again he heard the same sounds, not the same sounds at a different speed, but exactly the same sounds. He turned the tape over, wound it up backwards and pressed the play button again. The sounds were still there and they were still the same. It didn't sound backwards, or different, or sped-up or slowed down. No matter what he did to the tape, it played the same nonsensical combination of syllables and sounds.

To the dismay of ghost-hunters everywhere, this man had not an ounce of curiosity in his body. He simply bulk-erased the mysterious tape and continued on with his work as though nothing out of the ordinary had happened.

One theory about the haunting of this Edmonton-based radio station states that the ghost is the spirit of a young man killed in a motor vehicle accident. The station he's chosen to spend his eternity in is said to have been his favourite during his few years of life. The harmless, attention-getting pranks he plays seem adolescent enough to support such a possibility. In the meantime, it's a safe bet that the radio station staff occasionally credits Poltie with mysteries that their own absent-mindedness has actually caused. If they do, it seems to be all right with Poltie. By now he must be used to being the station's scapegoat.

CHAPTER 6

SPIRIT SNIPPETS

TRUCKERS HEAR SCREAMS

Almost exactly halfway between Calgary and Canmore, along the Trans-Canada Highway, at a spot known as Scott Lake Hill, there used to be a service station. It was set back a bit from the roadway and behind the station there was a neat little storey-and-a-half house where the owners lived. Tough economic times closed the business a few years ago and the shell of a building that had been the garage was demolished. The service road to and from the highway remained, however, as did the crumbling ruins of the house.

Long-distance truck drivers used to like to stop there to catch a few hours' sleep. The situation was ideal: a good, large pad of cement that was far enough off the road to be safe from oncoming traffic and yet not so far that the drivers would have to waste valuable time getting back to their route once they were rested.

Even the location was ideal for a rest stop. Having cleared Calgary, westbound drivers knew that most of the traffic congestion was behind them and that they had a good few kilometres to go before they were faced with the challenges of the mountain roads. Word spread quickly among the drivers and soon the site of the former garage became a popular, if unofficial, truck stop.

This popularity, however, didn't last long. One after another, the truckers who'd found the quiet lay-by stopped using it. A resident of Canmore explained that most of the truckers who stopped there only did so once. "Rumour had it that there'd been a rape on that property. The truckers said that as soon as they drifted off to sleep, they'd be aroused by the sounds of a woman's screams. The drivers would immediately jump out of their rigs and look around for the person in distress, but there was never anyone there. Before long it was commonly accepted that the place was haunted. No one pulls off the road there anymore," my informant conceded.

The house at Scott Lake Hill

THE GNOME

On a November evening in the early 1930s, Mary Bruce drove a buggy and a team of horses from the village of Glenevis to her family's farm. A naturally happy youngster, Mary entertained herself by singing "Red River Valley" as she made her way toward the warmth of home.

"As I approached the last leg of the drive, which meant going down a slight hill and up another before turning into our driveway, I saw a small figure coming toward me. I didn't pay too much attention to the figure as I was sure it was my kid sister coming to meet me," Mary explained. She went on to remark that not only was the figure about the same size as her sister, but it looked to be wearing a parka with a hood like her sister's and to be carrying a flashlight—possibly to guide Mary through the last bit of her journey.

"I became alarmed when the horses started to shy away and headed to the side of the road. The figure and I reached the hollow between the two hills at the same time. I tried to rein the horses to stop but they wouldn't," the woman remembered. "I still thought it was my sister. As the figure came even with the buggy, I looked down from the seat. It put its hand over the flashlight [and] I could see the red light [shining] between its fingers. Then it disappeared."

Both Mary and the horses were badly shaken by the sighting and so they covered the last half kilometre to home in record time.

"Dad wasn't pleased with me driving the horses so hard," she recounted, "but I leaped off the buggy and ran into the house to find my kid sister at the kitchen table doing her homework. The next day I went out to the hollow to see if there were any tracks in the dust. There were none."

The following Sunday, Mary visited one of her friends, the local school teacher. The two loved to frighten one another with scary tales, but in this case, Mary swore to herself that she wouldn't tell her friend of the experience in the hollow. Clearly, her friend hadn't made the same oath for she had a strange tale to tell Mary.

"As she was making coffee, she told me that the previous Thursday, as she came home from the neighbour's, she saw a small child standing on the doorstep of the teacherage. Then it vanished. My hair stood on end. Thursday was when I saw my apparition," Mary recalled.

They compared experiences and found them identical; they decided never again to tell stories of the unexplained.

AN ENCOUNTER WITH CHARLIE DUPRE?

I have no idea how Marcella Robe came to know my mailing address. I'm just glad she did or I might never have heard this story about the ghost of Charlie Dupre.

Marcella was heading for Vernon, British Columbia, but missed the bus that would have taken her there from Ghost Lake.

"I stood chilled to the bone," she described, remembering that it was about 8 o'clock in the evening and that her clothes, which might have been suitable during the day, were inadequate protection against the evening chill.

For two hours the woman waited in vain for someone to give her a ride. Discouraged, Marcella then gave up and made her way to a motel complex she'd spotted not far from the highway. She reported that as she walked towards the building, a man shuffled past her. She spoke to the man, asking for information about where the highway buses stopped. He didn't answer her, but just kept walking towards the gas-bar section of the establishment. Perhaps thinking that the stranger hadn't seen or heard her, Marcella tried to catch up to the man, but her legs were so cold that she suspects she wasn't moving as quickly as she would have liked to.

Despite her slowness, she and the man reached the door of the motel lobby at the same time.

"Please could you tell me the bus schedule?" she asked for a second time. Sensing that all was not well with the man, Marcella probed further. "What is your name?"

According to Marcella, the figure's answer came in a ghostly tremble and consisted of two words. The first word, "Charlie," was clear. The word that followed wasn't as clear, although the woman remembers hearing "Dup...something."

Then the figure walked past her and into the kitchen area. She noted at the time that no one in the dining room or kitchen area so much as looked up when the man walked through. Marcella, however, was more concerned with her own travel arrangements and as there was a motel employee in the lobby, Marcella explained her predicament and asked for directions.

She assumed that the man, now in the kitchen, who gave his name as Charlie, was also a lost traveler. She asked the desk clerk if he too, had made inquiries.

"What man?" came the puzzled reply.

"Why, the man who just walked through here into the kitchen. Didn't you see that man walk by?" she asked incredulously.

"No," he responded, with a tone of finality that didn't invite further questions.

Marcella used the facilities at the motel to arrange a ride to Vernon and to contact her relatives, letting them know she'd been delayed and that they shouldn't worry. She didn't, however, mention her strange encounter with a man only she appeared to be able to see.

"I could not even explain being stranded, never mind an encounter with a ghost!" she exclaimed.

PHONE-IN PHANTOMS

When I'm invited to be on the phone-in segment of television or radio talk shows, the calls usually come in hot and heavy. It seems that people are grateful for an opportunity to talk to someone who won't make fun of them for having had an experience with a ghost. Given the time restrictions on these shows, the best I can ever hope for is a few minutes for each retelling. As a result, the following stories are very short, but nevertheless intriguing.

⚘

The first caller on John Hanlon's *Wildrose Country* show was from Red Deer. He reported that at 3 PM on April 26, 1991, as he sat watching television, he felt certain that his grandfather had died. A few minutes later the phone rang. It was a relative calling with news that confirmed the man's feelings. His grandfather had, in fact, died just moments before.

⚘

A woman wanted to share an incident that had occurred in an Edmonton apartment building in 1991. She and her husband were awakened at 6:30 one morning by their alarm clock. Not unusual you say – no, except that neither she nor her husband had set the alarm and when she looked across the room she saw a little boy standing by the wall. The little figure ran toward the bed where the couple lay. He hit the ringing clock hard enough to break it.

"He had on a red-and-white striped shirt. He was kind of glowing and smirking at us," she explained. "When I turned around to look at him, he was gone. We've never seen him since."

⚜

A gentleman called to let us know about an incident that had occurred to his wife, Wendy, and her grandmother in the late 1960s. The two women had been out shopping and among other things bought six glass goblets. When they returned from their shopping trip, they decided to treat themselves to a snack. They set out a plate of cookies and poured milk into two of their newly purchased goblets. As Wendy walked across the kitchen floor, she slipped. One glass fell. They both watched as it hit the tile floor and broke. They were never able to find any trace of the milk that had been in the goblet, nor the pieces of broken glass.

⚜

An RCMP officer and his wife were stationed in the Northwest Territories; here is her tale: "Oftentimes when we went to bed at night or came in off a night shift, I'd say to him, 'Don't sleep too soundly because someone's going to die tonight.' This went on for the eight years we lived there. The last year we were in the Territories, on three different occasions within six weeks, I had said this to him and it always happened. He always got a call that there was a body. He said to me in March 1985, 'Don't ever say that again—don't ever tell me [that there's going to be a death.]'"

The caller went on to say that the premonitions of death recurred, but in keeping with her husband's request, she kept the information to herself. "The [premonitions have] happened in lots of different situations with me. Now I don't even say anything [about the feelings]," the woman concluded.

❧

A woman told of an experience that she had as a teenager while staying in Jasper, Alberta. She had gone to sleep for the night when something startled her into consciousness. She clearly saw two glowing figures at the foot of her bed. The luminescent apparitions then vanished before her eyes.

❧

A caller from Airdrie reported that her family had increased by more than just one when her son was born.

"The ghost was with us from 1980-87," she began. "[The haunting] began as soon as we brought our son home from the hospital. We would hear a baby crying when our baby wasn't."

This unseen infant traveled with the family, not only when they moved first from Calgary to Airdrie and then to a second house in Airdrie, but even when they went to Ontario to visit relatives.

"Our little guy [the ghost] got there before us," she said simply.

As their son aged, the ghostly pranks aged. The ghost began getting into the sorts of mischief one would expect from a toddler. As an example she explained that on more than one occasion they would find the telephone receiver had been taken off the hook. Once she found the freezer door open and an ice cream carton sitting on the stairs with a spoon beside it. "I knew it wasn't my son, because he was with me," she explained.

For a period of time the mother was concerned to note that her little boy appeared to be very tired every morning. He told her that the reason for his tiredness was that "the little boy who looks just like me keeps coming to the door and wanting to play with all my toys."

Eventually the occurrences became less and less frequent until eventually they stopped altogether. No one except her son actually saw the little ghost but both she and her husband were fully aware of its presence.

The caller had an interesting theory about the haunting. She wondered if her son had actually been an identical twin whose brother didn't develop in her womb. When her son was born, she explained, he was very small and the doctor apparently looked for another [baby to deliver]. The idea of the soul of a twin who didn't survive would explain the youngster referring to "the little boy who looks just like me."

As a final note, the caller reflected that "ever since he started school, all his friends have been twins."

❧

John Hanlon, the show's host, had this story to add to the collection. Bill Meilin, a professor in the drama department at the University of Alberta, is widely accepted as something of a local expert on the paranormal. Hanlon once took a course presented by Dr Meilin and remembers the professor recounting an incident that took place in the Meilin home during a social gathering.

Several couples got together for the evening. Their conversation must have included paranormal topics because they improvised a Ouija board in the hope of contacting a spirit. They did accomplish their purpose but the experience was far from a positive one.

The spirit who replied to their request for an audience was an arrogant one. He even took over the board's pointer to ask those gathered, "Are you afraid of me?" Showing more confidence than they probably felt, the group spelled out their answer, N-O. The spirit possessed the planchette a second time to mock the people by pointing to the letters H-A-H-A.

Mrs Meilin's patience had apparently reached its limit and she announced this would be the end of such parlour games. At that moment a piercing scream came from one of the children's bedrooms. Seconds later the entire group watched in horrified amazement as an unpleasant-looking man walked down the stairs and out the front door of the house.

When the screaming child calmed down somewhat, the group heard that the image had walked out of the child's closet, across the room and down the stairs.

❧

While enjoying being a part of a phone-in show on QR77 Radio in Calgary, I was told the following stories:

In the 1960s, while serving in the air force, a man named Alan told of climbing a radar tower to repair some receiver trouble. It surprised him to notice that another man, whom he wasn't expecting to be at work that night, was also up the tower. It was exactly midnight, not a likely time to come in to do a little extra work.

Alan greeted the man as he climbed, but received no reply. This lack of response struck Alan as being most extraordinary; however, he merely continued his attempt to fix the problem that had brought him to the tower. The next morning he discovered that the co-worker he'd seen at midnight and who hadn't replied to his greeting had been in a car accident that night. He had died from injuries he had received in the accident—at exactly midnight.

❧

Brenda told a story from the turn of the century. As a child, her grandfather had lived on a farm just outside Calgary. One day a fire started and the boy panicked. There were no adults around and he didn't know what to do. Should he run for his life or stay in the house, where he presumed his parents would come and get him. While he wondered what to do, a beautiful woman appeared out of nowhere and told him to "do what the pigs do." He knew that these animals run from fire and so he did so as well. That action no doubt saved the youngster's life, because the house burned to the ground and his parents wouldn't have been able to get to him. No one ever saw the woman who issued the advice either before or since.

❧

Wendy spoke of a couple of strange incidents that took place in her home during the early 1980s. Wendy still lives in the house and reports that by now she just accepts an unseen woman's presence as normal for her home.

Both the kitchen taps and lights would turn on when no one was near them and as Wendy lay on the chesterfield watching television, she would suddenly feel a cold breeze blow across her legs and then back across in the opposite direction. When she looked into the history of her house, she found that years before a woman had stabbed herself to death in it.

⚜

I was delighted when Dave Kormos, news director at Medicine Hat's CJCY radio station, invited me to participate on John Hamill's *Hotline* show just before Halloween in 1995. As usual, the calls were fascinating. The first caller was a woman, who began her conversation matter-of-factly. "We've had a ghost with us for two years now," she said. "It started with children playing with a Ouija board and calling back their favorite dead uncle. It began with minor occurrences such as balls bouncing, [and us hearing the] swish, swishing of [his] coveralls.

As she progressed in relating her story, it became clear that not only had the strength of the haunting increased, but so had her concern about the situation. "By now it's very visible to most family members. There's never anything threatening about the presence. I'm sure it is the uncle," she confided. Despite all these reassurances, the woman was legitimately concerned about what the spirit's intentions might be.

"As it's becoming stronger, I have contacted local ministers. They say it's real and will have to deal with it by the power of prayer," was how she ended her story.

⚜

The old Patterson armory in Medicine Hat is widely accepted as being haunted. The place, which host John Hamill described as a great, cavernous building, was used during the Second World War as a prisoner-of-war camp for captured Germans. There is documentation to prove that during that time it was the site of an execution. An inmate was apparently hanged by his fellow prisoners for divulging information. It is widely presumed that his is the spirit that haunts the old place.

Two callers had personal experiences to verify the rumours. The first man identified himself as Mr X.

"I've been there lots of times," he explained. "I'm a very spiritual person and have seen this ghost in there. He'll usually walk from one end of the promenade to the other."

Mr X has been so convinced that there actually was someone up there that he has gone up and checked around but no one was there. The area he described was where the prisoners had hanged the man more than fifty years ago.

The next caller asked to be referred to as Mr Y. He too was associated with the armories and although he has never seen anything, he explained that working alone late at night in the building can be hard on the nerves.

"You sure hear a lot of strange noises, loud banging noises, footsteps, doors closing," he acknowledged. "The other night I was working and I heard 'Bang, bang, bang.' I went and checked and there was nothing but I heard it again. There was still nothing there. "

Mr Y apparently takes some consolation in the theory that a ghost will not stray from its haunt into a newly added part of the building. "The joke around here is [that] if you see the ghost, just run for the new part of the building," he said.

❧

The on-air telephone calls even inspired a radio station employee to share an experience he'd had four years before.

Jay stated that one incident "totally changed my whole outlook. I was skeptical [until] friends and I were at a bonfire. Someone had a Ouija board. What happened totally freaked me out. We were mocking the people who were playing it. I [decided to] ask it some questions that only I would know the answers to."

"What's my middle name?" Jay had inquired of the board, sure that no one in his group of friends would have any way of knowing the answer to that question.

"It spelled it wrong but it was the same name," Jay explained. "Then I asked it the birth date of my grandpa and [the board] got it." He recalled how he began to think, "This is real."

Jay needed further proof though, so he asked about something he knew no person outside his immediate family would be able to answer. "My mother had a baby that passed away when it was an infant and the board knew the baby's name," he noted.

That was enough for Jay. His final question was "Who are you?"

"It spelled D-E-V-I-L," he recalled. "I got into my car and I got out of there as fast as I could. I couldn't sleep for two weeks after that. I'll tell you, that one experience changed my whole attitude."

Even over the phone lines, the tension in Jay's voice as he related the story was evident. This was clearly a man who'd had a profound and moving encounter.

❧

The next caller, Floyd, spoke of a promise his father-in-law made to him just after he married the man's daughter, Gerry: "He told me that if I ever mistreated his daughter, he would come back to haunt me. Shortly after that, my father-in-law died and shortly after that I got into a very heated argument with my wife," he remembered.

He left the house in anger and went to a local pub where he ordered two beers.

"That was when I saw my father-in-law. He was in his railway uniform and I had never seen him dressed that way," the caller said. "Just as I saw him, a friend came over to my table and stepped into the ghost. The guy looked at me and said, 'Floyd, what's wrong? You're as white as a sheet.' I ran home with my hair standing on end."

"A couple of nights later, my wife and I walked into the bar. A friend came over to our table and said, 'I saw Gerry's dad the other night.' I asked him when and he told me it was 9:35. That was exactly the time that I saw him."

Floyd's friend, however, had spotted the apparition while he was out on a tractor working his land. "He was in the furrows in my field," the man explained.

After that, Gerry's deceased father kept a close eye on the newlywed couple. "We would hear him upstairs or in a rocking chair," he reported. "Finally we said, 'Dad, for God's sake, leave us alone,' and that was the end of it."

Presumably Gerry's father is confident enough in her marriage that he has gone on to his final rest.

⚜

The next caller began by saying hers was a "pleasant story, one that warms your cockles." She described how her mother-in-law had died in January of 1989 and her own mother the following November.

"One morning the whole family was sleeping. I got up at the usual time, just before dawn, and went in to wake my daughter up. When I did, she asked me if I'd just been into her room a little while ago. I told her no, that I was sleeping. She said, 'Mom there was a lady sitting on the foot of the bed and I thought it was you.'"

When the caller asked her daughter what the lady looked like, the child was ready with the description. The youngster said, "She was slight in build, about your height, Mom. She was just sitting there watching over me. She didn't frighten me. She didn't bother me at all. I just rolled over and went back to sleep."

The caller wondered who her daughter's visitor had been. The child's description of the apparition seemed to rule out the caller's own mother and eventually they reached the conclusion that it was her mother-in-law who had sat with her daughter so early that morning.

"My mother-in-law and my daughter were close. I think she came to her to see that everything was all right before she went on her way to wherever," the caller concluded.

The little girl seems to have accepted this explanation too and simply says, "My nana came to say goodbye to me."

⚜

Tammy, the next caller, now lives in Medicine Hat but her encounter with the spirit world occurred while she lived in Calgary.

"I have kind of a story," she began. "It's pretty freaky what happened. I was living with my boyfriend for two or three years in Calgary. He was in a car accident. Before he died, he promised that he would be with me always."

No doubt missing him dreadfully, Tammy and some of her friends decided to try to contact the recently deceased man by using a Ouija board.

"We set out the candles and everything like you're supposed to, but when the board started moving, we got scared and stopped. The next morning I could smell bacon and eggs. We used to have bacon and eggs every morning for breakfast, and after he would sit on the couch with his robe on and read the paper. [On this morning after the seance] I went to the kitchen and grabbed a cup of tea. I came into the living room and he was sitting there on my couch, in his robe. I didn't know what to do. I started to cry and I turned around. When I looked back he was gone," she remembered. "I'm still shaking just talking about it. He had a white glow around him. I got a good look at him for maybe two or three minutes."

Tammy ended the story by acknowledging somewhat wistfully that she hadn't felt his presence since then.

❧

The last caller was a woman named Pat. She reported that when she was 18 and her grandmother was 81, the older woman died.

"The evening of the funeral I was in my bedroom in the basement and I was thinking about the events of the day. The coffin appeared in the corner of the room and I could see my grandmother in it. She sat up. She looked scared and put out her arms to me."

Pat was understandably badly frightened by the image and ran upstairs to get her dog for company. However, she described the result as follows: "Normally he loved to sleep with me, but this time he wouldn't stay."

From all I've been told about the sensitivity of animals to the presence of spirits, that final aspect of the story didn't surprise me at all. What is unusual about Pat's story—and makes it even more poignant than most such tales—is that this sort of a sighting is usually comforting to a grieving relative, not deeply disturbing in the way Pat's encounter clearly was.

CHAPTER 7

HOLY GHOSTS
& SCHOOLS

THE ENCHANTED COTTAGE

In order to protect the current owner's real estate investment, the people who shared this story with me have asked only to be identified by the pseudonyms Sam and Sue. The property where this ghost story took place is an unusual one and therefore easily recognized, so I have accepted their request with understanding.

The couple's haunted home was situated in central Calgary, on the same property as a considerably larger residence that was associated with a religious organization. The cottage was also very haunted. But even without its ghost, Sam explained, it was a special place.

"In many ways it was an enchanted cottage," Sam explained, adding that he had already lived there for some time before he and Sue married. And it was during those first few years that Sam's father agreed to let Sam take his piano from the family home in Bowden to his new home, the Calgary cottage.

Sam's parents had bought the used piano directly from the manufacturer in 1948, the year he was born. They hoped their son would grow up playing and enjoying the instrument. Their wish came true – Sam became an accomplished pianist. When he left home, however, Sam's father was somewhat hesitant to let the young man take the lovely old Heintzman with him to Calgary. Perhaps it was the older man's way of keeping a little piece of his son at home. Eventually, however, Sam's father relented.

"I finally convinced my dad to let me have the piano. This was quite exciting and the day it arrived one of the women [who lived in the larger residence on the property] came over to see it. She stopped cold in her tracks. 'That's my piano,' she said."

The woman explained that as a young woman she had been something of a pianist. In 1947, when it became apparent that her life was going to head in another direction, she had sold her beloved piano back to the manufacturer, Heintzman.

"It was the one possession I regretted giving up and now God's brought it right back to me," she told Sam with utter amazement. From that day on, the two shared the old Heintzman in its new enchanted home.

While that arrangement pleased both Sam and the neighbour, the piano was not nearly as well received by the resident ghost.

"One night I really ticked her off," Sam told me. He then described one night when he came home from work late and decided to practise for a while. "I was playing a Rachmaninoff piece. It was really tricky."

In order to master the composition, Sam had been going over and over a few bars. By 4 AM the spirit had apparently had enough.

"I heard her coming downstairs and she slammed the door," Sam remembered. "I told her, 'I'm sorry but I've got to get this piece right.'"

Oddly, in the four years the ghost never appeared to Sam, although she did to some other people. He did, however, become well acquainted with her routine and after a few months he realized that every second Wednesday evening she would visit the larger house next door. This was the ghost's turn to disturb Sam's sleep.

"I'd be in bed around midnight and I'd hear the doors open and close and hear her coming up the stairs."

The first time these noises occurred, Sam responded by arming himself with a baseball bat, but when nothing appeared, he realized it was just his resident ghost. After that he knew to expect the late night noises every other Wednesday.

"We had our positives. We lived fairly happily together," Sam said referring to his invisible roommate.

One of those positives was an unexpected serenade during a dinner party Sam was giving. As he was preparing the meal and chatting with his guests the little group began to hear a violin being played downstairs.

"I went beetling downstairs but there was no one there and the music stopped. I went back upstairs and it started again," Sam remembered. Next he got the guests involved in attempting to solve the musical mystery.

"We all went downstairs. It was minus 25 or 30 degrees outside. We split up and checked all around outside but there was nobody out there." Despite this search, the group was serenaded by phantom violin music throughout dinner.

Sam and Sue began their married life living in the haunted house. Sam worked nights and wanted to be sure his new bride would be safe at home in his absence so he and his father set about reinforcing locks and securing windows. As is often the case in haunted buildings, the renovations caused the spirit's activity level to increase dramatically.

"She took the changes as a real challenge," Sam recalled.

The ghost's most spectacular stunt, however, was still to come, and when it did it led Sam to the find of a lifetime. "I was sitting watching television when I heard a gunshot. It went right past my ear," he elaborated. "I crept over to the window and crawled around trying to investigate [where the shot had come from]."

Although the area around the house appeared to be deserted, Sam went out into the yard to investigate further. There was no one there and despite his best efforts he couldn't find evidence that anyone had even been on the property recently. He went back inside and decided instead to search for proof that the shot had actually occurred.

Carefully following the path that a bullet would have taken after whizzing past his right ear, Sam found himself at a far wall. Because the second storey of the house was under the gable, there had been a false wall installed some years before. Although he couldn't see any bullet hole, he decided to open the door he discovered in the false wall to see if he could find the spent cartridge there.

He didn't. He did, however, find a violin.

"I went racing over to show [the women in the larger house]. They said I was welcome to keep it, so I showed it to a friend of mine. The violin had been made in 1721 and according to her it was a good one, well worth fixing up. I think the gun shot that I was investigating might have been the ghost's way of showing me that the violin was there."

After a number of years of living in the unique and very haunted house, Sam and Sue moved on but neither of them has ever forgotten their experiences in the enchanted cottage.

"At Halloween, when the newspapers run stories about haunted houses, we just laugh. They report one or two instances but, for us, in that house, it was an everyday thing, a way of life."

Sam considers the long-lasting effects the residency had on the couple as being positive. He spoke of how both he and Sue lost the cynicism they had developed over the years and how they were revitalized by living with dramatic proof that there is an after-life.

At the moment, Sam and Sue's former home is tied up with the complications inherent in settling an estate. It is to be hoped that the legal proceedings won't have upset the poor soul who has chosen to make this enchanted cottage her very permanent home.

THE DUNVEGAN RECTORY

There are many theories that attempt to explain what a ghost is or why a place might be haunted. Some say that a ghost is a psychic imprint left behind by the energy of the deceased. Others feel the phenomenon emanates from the subconscious of the individual who is experiencing it. At least one parapsychologist is convinced that most hauntings can be explained by the theory of retrocognition, which purports that people encountering a ghost have become temporarily displaced from their usual place in time.

While it is difficult to believe that any single theory, no matter how ambitious, could hope to explain every ghostly encounter, the story of the Dunvegan rectory appears to strongly support retrocognition as a possible explanation. Perhaps this case even requires retrocognition to explain the otherwise unexplainable.

The following events took place during July 1992, at the Dunvegan Historic Site in northwestern Alberta. On the shores of the majestic Peace River, the site was a Catholic mission and fur-trading centre during the 1800s.

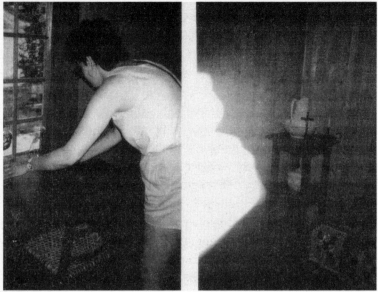

Dunvegan Rectory

Now a picturesque spot, the place has been restored to reflect those early days. A visit to Dunvegan offers a unique opportunity to step back in time and explore life as it was when the church and the ort buildings were new. At least two visitors, mother and daughter Gayle and Janice Moon, unwittingly took that opportunity literally and experienced an exhausting and disorienting period of apparent retrocognition.

The family's plans for the day hadn't included a trip to the rectory. As a matter of fact, Gayle and her husband, Neil, along with Janice and her daughter, Kelsey, had already enjoyed a full family day picking strawberries. They were all thirsty after the berry picking, however, and knew they could find drinking fountains at the site. They arrived at the Dunvegan buildings around 8 PM on July 11, 1992.

"We really had no intention of looking at the site, as we were just having a drink and planning on leaving," Janice began animatedly. "We had no idea that...day was the grand opening [for the restored site]. We heard the bells ring and saw two interpreters in period costume walking toward the back of the rectory. Mom and I just continued walking toward the site, with Dad and Kelsey following."

In her quest to satisfy her thirst, Janice Moon was blissfully unaware that she was about to embark on the experience of a lifetime. As her parents went into the church, Janice took her daughter's hand and walked to a statue of a woman that had caught her eye.

"[It] was stark, no plaque or inscription. I immediately felt shivers, walked around her two or three times looking for identification and [felt] frustrated because there was none," Janice explained. "I kept looking at her face but was afraid to touch her."

Finally, with a great force of will, Janice reached out and touched the stone-cold hem of the figure's robe. The uncomfortable feelings increased. "I had completely forgotten about Kelsey, even though she was still with me," Janice commented.

Just then, Janice's mother came back out of the church. Although they didn't know it at the time, both mother and daughter were experiencing equally bizarre reactions to the religious icons around them.

"Mom felt overwhelmed by the paintings in the church. [She] came out and walked over to us," Janice recounted. "Mom looked at the statue and said, 'Where did she come from?' Mom was positive she had never seen her before, even though she had been to Dunvegan several times over the years."

Like her daughter, Gayle Moon felt hesitant to touch the statue. To her the inanimate object had taken on ominous qualities.

"The statue was eerie," Gayle recalled. "Bordering on being very threatening. I couldn't look at her eyes. I couldn't look at her face. I had visited the site many times and I had never seen the statue [before] although Neil has informed me that the statue has been there for years."

As Janice had, Gayle eventually brought herself to touch the statue but even as she did, Gayle wondered at the marble it had been made from, for the stone seemed luminous. Moments later, the three generations of women walked away from the sculpture, but the strange sensations Janice and Gayle were experiencing weren't that easy to leave behind.

"We walked past the church. I stopped and looked at a dark-haired interpreter who was standing inside the church door," Janice remembered. She certainly wasn't aware of it then, but the sensitive Janice was no longer perceiving her surroundings as other people around her were. "He was no longer in costume but in grey dress pants with black flecks. I felt he was dressed wrong for who he really was."

Gayle's thoughts were equally as odd. She had noticed the interpreter earlier and thought, "He knows and he's a real part of this history."

Both Janice's and Gayle's thought processes were beginning to reflect their shift in chronological perspective from present to past. Their immediate surroundings were becoming vague and distant. Two site interpreters in period costume passed the women and spoke to them.

"I heard them but they seemed very far away," Janice mused, adding, "I was not aware of Kelsey, other people or noises."

The little group made their way into the rectory. Gayle walked over to the altar. Janice reported that her mother "had a very strong feeling that she was in someone's home, [that] they weren't there and [that] she had no business being there, [that] she was imposing."

The women's perception of reality was now alternating from present to past. Gayle's feelings were intensified when she saw the altar. "There was something wrong with the green cloth on the altar. It was too much green. There was no white cloth over the green cloth," Gayle recalled. She also felt that the candlesticks on the altar were out of place.

While Janice was bothered by the same objects as her mother was, the younger woman's sensations had, by this time, become physiological.

"I felt a strong sense of tingling through my body. I had a strong feeling of someone there," Janice said. "I made a comment about too much green cloth. I looked at the candlesticks, which were all lined up against the far shelf of the altar and knew [that they were] wrong. We turned around and both walked into the back bedroom under the stairs."

They found out later that this room was known as the Priest's Room. Gayle remarked how she "saw the bed, the wardrobe against the wall and the clothes hanging up on a wooden clothes hanger with hooks."

More than just Gayle's sense of sight was becoming involved, though; she reported that she had "smelled a warm body smell as if someone had just gotten out of bed." The feeling of intruding on someone's personal space was increasing.

"Mom felt really uncomfortable and intrusive, not threatened but just that she was somewhere she wasn't supposed to be," Janice reported on Gayle's behalf.

The effect on Janice, normally down-to-earth, was even more dramatic – the present had all but slipped away.

"From the doorway I looked at the clothes and said to myself with relief, 'Thank God he hung them up properly!' I knew in my heart that someone had just taken those clothes off. I then turned toward the bed, having no idea where Mom was in the room. I had the sense that someone was in bed," Janice said.

The bed was protected by a surround of mosquito netting that Janice felt drawn to touch. As she did, a near-panic overtook her. "I became overwhelmed with a strong tingling sensation throughout my whole body. I said, 'Get me out of here!' Mom heard me and followed me out of the room as I left immediately," said the younger woman by way of describing her troubled flight from the room.

After returning briefly to the altar and once again being bothered by the solid green cloth, Janice made her way into another bedroom in the rectory.

"I glanced in, not paying attention to what I saw, turned around and saw Kelsey. I asked her if she wanted to go upstairs. She said 'Yes, do you?'" Janice agreed to go with her daughter, but noted that "[My] mom could not bring herself to go upstairs as she felt this was private and she'd had enough."

Janice herself felt almost equally uncomfortable about going upstairs, but she had told Kelsey she would accompany her. When she looked up the stairs she could see that other people were visiting the area and she felt somewhat foolish about her concerns of a moment earlier.

Janice and Kelsey made their way up the stairs and, for a few minutes anyway, into a more comfortable part of Janice's trip through time. She recalled that the staircase was narrow, but that the steps were not worn.

"By the time I reached the top of the stairs, I felt totally at ease and peaceful; all apprehension was gone," Janice noted. At the top of the stairs the pair turned right and Janice informed her daughter that this was the Trapper's Room. Here the strange sensations continued but at least now they were pleasant and easy to cope with.

"I became excited when I saw the window to the right of the door. I opened it, explaining to Kelsey how it opened. It was very easy to open…. The window felt cool and smooth. I looked outside for an instant and it was quiet outside. I saw nothing. I lost Kelsey's presence but knew she was there. We walked into the room across the hall. I told Kelsey this was the Student's Room," Janice remembered. Those recent pleasant feelings were instantly replaced by intensely unpleasant ones, for now even her personal identity was becoming caught up in the time warp.

"I was instantly angry and said to myself, 'You work so hard and there isn't even a net over your bed.' I was still talking to Kelsey but when we left this room I lost her completely. We walked across the empty hall area and into the far corner bedroom. At the doorway I saw the desk in front of the window," Janice described. "I turned…to the desk and sitting on it was the bottom half of an oil lamp, then the top half of the oil lamp, then the clear glass inkwell with a solid blue smooth wooden pen with the black tip resting in the inkwell. I was very calm and totally absorbed within myself, not hearing or seeing anyone. I touched the bottom half of the lamp and then the top half. I picked up the pen with my left hand and held it up by my shoulder, my arm bent."

That simple movement caused the apparition to appear.

"Immediately I was standing directly behind a man, a priest with his hat and jacket on. He was sitting at the desk, writing with the blue pen with his right hand. The oil lamp was together and lit, sitting in the left corner of the desk. I looked at the window and saw it was dark outside.

I looked back at the priest—he was still writing and sitting straight in his chair with only his head bent forward. I could see the top half of the pen and the top of [one of his] knuckles. Even though he had his hat on, I could see his beard on either side of his head," she recalled.

"His beard was bushy but soft to touch and it was brown with a reddish tinge to it. I felt that it was right that I was there – I belonged there and it was so peaceful!

"I don't know how long I stood there with him but [eventually] I realized what was happening. I shrieked or gasped and threw the pen. It landed back in its original place in the inkwell. From far away I heard Kelsey say, 'Mommy, do you think you broke the pen?' I said 'No,' turned to see her and she was gone. I was shaking. I looked up out the window and saw daylight. I glanced around the room feeling very shaken and scared and knew I had to get out. I was spooked completely and felt that I was losing my mind. I started down the stairs as quickly as I could," continued Janice.

At the bottom of the stairs, Gayle Moon was concerned as she watched her daughter hurrying down the steps. Janice had undergone reconstructive surgery to both knees and for this reason normally walked down stairs slowly and carefully. Gayle knew that something must be provoking Janice in order for her to be rushing on such a set of stairs. Like Janice, Gayle could see that the steps were narrow but the older woman could also see that they were badly enough worn to be worthy of at least a little extra care. Janice, however, was still experiencing retrocognition, viewing things as they had been more than a hundred years ago. To her, the stairs were not hazardously worn but new and even.

"Halfway down the stairs, I became aware of other people walking around. I panicked, as I wanted Kelsey and I out of the rectory now! We walked away from the rectory and sat down on a bench. I was very quiet and watched everyone else to see if they were normal. They walked by laughing and talking," she noted, commenting that even though she was now outside, she was still feeling tremendously shaken and disoriented. "Without looking at Mom I said, 'I saw a man upstairs.

I saw a priest writing at the desk upstairs.' Mom was not surprised and that made me feel okay."

Slowly, Janice's mental and emotional states returned to normal. Because Gayle's feeling of intruding on someone's privacy had prevented her from going upstairs, her readjustment to here and now came somewhat more quickly. Even so, the two women were badly shaken and stayed up until the wee hours of the morning discussing their experiences.

Both of them realized that no matter how much talking they did, they would have to return to the restored buildings at Dunvegan in order to properly assess their ordeal. In the meantime, Janice tried to sort out her experiences in her mind.

"I was willing to admit that I'd seen a ghost but I was just befuddled and emotionally distraught when I realized that what I'd seen on the 11th [of July] isn't really what you see when you go in there," Janice recalled. Unfortunately, that contradiction was going to be a fact she would also have to come to grips with. The family returned to the mission buildings on July 19th.

"We started at the statue again and I was sorely disappointed, because the stone did not look the same. It had lost its lustre. It was just stone," Gayle said.

Next they made their way back to the rectory. Peter, the interpreter assigned to the house that day, was busy with other visitors and so Gayle and Janice began to look about on their own.

"I think we unnerved [Peter] a bit because we looked at each other and said, 'It's changed, it's been changed.'" Gayle remembered.

They were sure the quilt on the bed in the priest's room was different than it had been on their previous visit. Janice became very agitated because the hat that she thought should be on the rack in that room wasn't there. She also noted a red trunk or chest on the floor and commented, "That wasn't there on the 11th or I'd have fallen over it."

Gayle remarked that an oil lamp she knew she'd seen on a wall was not only gone but there was no trace of it ever having been. There was no mark on the wall where it would have been, nor any stains from the smoke or soot.

When they went upstairs both Gayle and Janice felt that there had been even more changes. Janice tried to open the window as she had on her previous visit. It had been smooth and new and easy to open that day. Today it was old and very difficult to open.

There were desks and bookcases in the central part of the second floor, which both women maintained hadn't been there when they'd visited only a few days before. It was in the visiting bishop's room that they noted the greatest number of changes.

"They've moved the bed, they've moved the picture, they've moved a lot of this stuff and the net is gone," Janice informed her mother on their second visit. From the tone in her voice it was clear that these differences were extremely bothersome to the younger woman.

Gayle realized that her daughter was really emotionally distraught over all of this and that her voice was getting louder and louder. When she heard someone come up the stairs, she went to the head of the staircase to greet the person she hoped it would be, Peter.

"I thought, 'This fellow will need some warning about what's happening,' so I stopped him in the hallway and asked him some questions. I said, 'How many spirits have you encountered in this place?'" she recounted.

The interpreter was somewhat taken aback, but replied candidly: "Well, none as such, but we have had strange happenings. There have been times when we've closed the window on the north side of the central second floor and [later] found it open and other times we've opened the window and [later] found it closed. Sometimes we're downstairs and we hear footsteps upstairs."

His reply gave Gayle the opportunity she needed to give the young man some details of her family's decidedly unusual visit just a few days before. "We've come back today to look for answers," she concluded.

Thus forewarned, Peter went with Gayle to join Janice, who immediately accused the interpreter of moving things around at the site. With a surprised look, Peter replied that, no, nothing has been moved here. Janice, of course, couldn't accept that and she began to enumerate the changes. She informed him that not only had the bed been moved but the mosquito netting that had hung around it on the 11th was now missing.

"There's never been any netting around that bed," Peter assured the concerned Janice. "There isn't even anything to hang it from."

Gayle countered by pointing to the ceiling beams over where her daughter had insisted that the bed was located during her July 11th visit. Sure enough, there were nail holes in a pattern from which, many years ago, mosquito netting could have hung.

Janice's level of concern had escalated by now. Deeply upset by the differences she was observing, she handed her purse and camera to her mother and began to cry. Gayle took two or three pictures and then left her daughter alone awhile to settle down. When those photographs were developed the women were in for the surprise of their lives. Two snaps were taken just seconds apart, with barely any camera movement. The first one shows Janice re-arranging artifacts to where she was sure they should have been placed. To take the second picture her mother moved the camera only slightly to the right but that frame captured a stark, white form hovering behind Janice as she made the adjustments she felt necessary.

"You can see [by that photo] that he was right there with me," Janice explained, now many months later.

Peter suggested that they call Kelsey in to show them where she thought the bed had been on their last visit. The little girl joined them moments later and with great assuredness pointed to the area where her mother had said she'd seen the bed. She also described the netting but then became nervous, uncomfortable and uncommunicative.

"She'd had enough," her grandmother assessed.

When the group went back downstairs Janice noticed a hat in the common room and called out, "There's the hat. That hat was on the rack in the bedroom."

"No," Peter advised. "It's always been right there."

In the priest's room both Gayle and Janice remarked that the wardrobe was now missing. To which Peter replied, "There's never been a wardrobe in this room."

There was now a white cloth covering the green cloth on the altar. On the 11th both women had remarked that there was no contrasting colour to break the solid green. Peter tried to explain that there was a set way to dress the altar and that it had looked exactly the same for many years.

Janice asked to see any old photographs that might be at the site. She wanted to see if she could spot the priest that she'd seen on her first visit. Peter brought some archival photos to her, but she was sure none of the men pictured in the shots showed the man she'd seen. When her mother suggested that she had perhaps seen someone other than a priest, Janice became very indignant. She knew who she'd seen; now it was just a matter of finding a picture of him so that she could identify him.

Peter was more than patient with Janice's challenges. "You don't work in a place like this without an open mind," he acknowledged. He then explained that he had a very ritualized procedure that he went through each night as he locked up. He called it "putting the house to bed."

All of Peter's co-workers knew how conscientious he was when he closed the house for the evening. For this reason, once a co-worker was surprised to see a light on in the visiting bishop's room, even though it was long past the time the house would normally be dark.

"He was quite a ways away when he saw it, but he drove over here to investigate," Peter told them. "When he got to the rectory, he could see that there was no light on and that the curtains were closed."

Janice and Gayle were somewhat helped by their second visit, combined with Peter's stories. At least now they knew they weren't the only ones to have had strange experiences at Dunvegan. Still, that return trip wasn't quite enough and the family returned for the third time on July 26th. By then word of their bizarre trip through time had spread and so they were instantly recognized and welcomed when they returned.

Both Gayle and Janice spent a large part of the visit going over what they felt were the changes that they had noted. The staff listened intently and surmised that perhaps the historians responsible for the site had unwittingly erred in re-creating the rooms.

The seriousness with which the historic site's staff took Janice's assessments shocked her nearly as much as her trip back in time had. "I was just amazed to be taken so seriously," Janice commented, regarding the alterations that were made to Dunvegan based on her retrocognitive experience in the summer of 1992.

This extraordinary ghost story has a very tender ending. A few months after visiting the site and having the incredible experience, Janice Moon was at home in Edmonton, asleep in bed, when she distinctly felt a kiss being placed on her cheek.

"I knew it was him, the priest that I'd seen on July 11. He'd come to say good-bye," she affirmed.

By informing the staff of the differences between what she saw while she was experiencing retrocognition and what she saw on subsequent visits, Janice had helped the long-dead priest execute the changes he needed to make before he could be released from his earthbound haunt.

Now at last, thanks to his successful communication with Janice Moon, the unidentified priest was free to move on to his final reward.

THE CHURCH THAT WOULDN'T BE PHOTOGRAPHED

Margaret Smith, an insurance adjuster in Calgary, had a strange tale to tell. While it was not strictly a ghost story, it is certainly as mystifying as one.

A vehicle collision had occurred in a back lane. As part of her investigation, Margaret was required to shoot photographs of the scene.

"[The accident] had happened at a T intersection in an alley. There was a church at the top end of the T. I took shots of all three sides," she explained. She was using an instant-processing camera and film, so she merely laid each shot on the seat of the car to finish developing as she went on to the next photo. "I thought I was through, but when I checked the pictures, only two had developed. The third one, the one of the church at the top of the T, was blank. I figured that particular frame of the film was defective so I took another shot and waited for it to develop. It didn't develop either."

Not wanting to waste time, Margaret changed the entire roll of film and took another picture of the church.

"That one was blank too," Margaret said.

The young woman left the site without ever having completely accomplished her purpose. It seemed as though the church simply did not want its picture taken.

ORGANIST'S
AMAZING EXPERIENCE

James Cornock had an amazing ghost story to tell and the way he told it indicated an amazing attitude toward his experience.

"I wasn't scared. It was more a feeling of wonderment. Actually it was a pretty neat experience," he explained quietly.

James is the organist at Knox Church in Calgary and has been for eight to ten years. Until recently, though, he had no idea the place was haunted.

"It was very odd that day," he acknowledged. In all his years with the church, the subject of ghosts or hauntings had never come up, even though James spoke frequently with other staff members, especially the church secretary, Jeanie, who had worked there for thirty years.

"One day I was at the pipe organ, practising," he continued. "I was the only person in the sanctuary." James explained that there was a wall of oak panelling behind him with roughly a 15 centimetre space between the panels.

As he concentrated on learning the piece, James became aware that he was no longer alone. Someone or something had joined him. It had come through the gap in the panelling. He knew immediately that whatever it was couldn't be human, as no person could have slipped through such a small opening. Despite this realization, he knew that a presence had joined him.

"Something came up behind me. It passed behind me. There was a presence there," he emphasized. "There was a shape there and the air was heavier. It looked at the [sheet] music, then it kept going. It nonchalantly exited by the choir exit behind the console. I wasn't afraid, more shocked."

James's description of the apparition was amazingly detailed. He described a 1.8 metre tall man in his late 60s. "He was really opaque, faint. There was a mass there, though, because I did feel it."

Despite the decidedly unusual experience, James continued his practice session as planned. "I kept playing for about half an hour and then went to turn the key in [to the church secretary]," he confirmed.

The interaction with the woman he'd known for the better part of ten years puzzled him as much as the form passing through the sanctuary had. "Jeanie and I had never brought this subject up before," he recalled, "but on that day she asked me, 'Have you ever seen a ghost here?'"

Astounded that she would pick this particular day to ask such a question, James described the presence he'd just witnessed. The woman was not surprised. Apparently the spirit whose presence James felt is only one of the two ghosts who make their home in the church.

The concept of a haunted church is certainly not unique to this one in Calgary. For example, there are a multitude of ghost stories surrounding the old abbeys and cathedrals in the British Isles. The oddity of this story is the coincidence of Jeanie's direct question concerning a never-before discussed topic immediately after James's first-ever experience.

Perhaps now, given James's positive attitude towards his first encounter, and his and Jeanie's shared awareness of the spectres in their church, the spirits will make themselves felt more often.

HE WHISTLES
WHILE HE WORKS

Some months ago I was invited to spend a day doing readings and chatting with the students at two schools in a pretty little town in south-central Alberta. In the morning I arrived to a warm greeting at the high school. Before beginning the first session, I was invited to join the teachers for coffee in the staff room. Everyone was very friendly and many people made a point to come over and chat with me. A few of them indicated that they might have an additional ghost story for me—right there in the school. The day was certainly starting out well!

Sadly, those enticing leads were all I was able to come away with. No one, it seemed, really knew the story. Everyone had just heard that there was such a story. I decided that the high school ghost story was most likely little more than a legend created over the years by generations of students. Despite this disappointing realization, I spent a most enjoyable morning at the high school and found the students to be as welcoming as their teachers were.

After lunch, I went on to the junior high school in town. Again I was warmly received and again I was given to understand that the school was haunted. Given the frustrations I had experienced trying to pin down this morning's potential ghost story, I decided not to let the possibility of a new lead distract me from reading to the students. I spent a delightful afternoon reading and talking to group after group of students.

As I left, I was told the principal wanted to see me. It seemed he was well aware of the ghost story connected with his school. Not only had he felt and heard the spirit on several occasions, he even thought he'd caught a glimpse of the spectre walking past the door of the school's office when he knew he was alone in the building. His encounters were nothing though, he informed me, compared to those experienced by a member of the school's caretaking staff. I made a note to follow up on this enticing lead in the coming months.

When I began the research for this book, I contacted the people associated with all the leads I'd collected over the years. Phoning that junior high school principal was one of the priorities on my agenda. Unfortunately, he didn't return my phone calls. I was, however, able to track down the custodian, Liz. She had quite a story to tell.

She had worked at the school for nearly twenty years and indicated that she'd been aware of the presence pretty well since she started.

"The only thing I can really say is that often I can hear keys and I hear footsteps in the area downstairs by the staff room. Years back, when I was waxing the floors, I heard whistling," she related.

Not so unusual, you might think – except that Liz knew for a fact that when she heard the whistling she was alone. She had locked herself in at the otherwise empty school.

"One other morning I had just punched in the security code and I heard coughing," she explained, before assuring me that no one could have been in the school ahead of her without first turning off the alarm that she had just deactivated. Upon entering the school, she found it as empty as she had expected it would be. Despite it being empty, she remained convinced of what she'd heard.

"When you're by yourself in the school, you feel a presence. You feel someone's watching you," Liz said. "[Nevertheless,] I feel safe. It's friendly. It's come to the point where I don't even think much about it."

Some time after the current principal took on his new school assignment there, he became suspicious that not everything was normal, so Liz was the one he approached with his concerns. Perhaps because she had been associated with the school for so long, he made a point to ask her one day, "Is there a ghost in the school?"

Liz explained as best she could about George, while acknowledging that she had absolutely no theories about who the spirit might actually be or why he hasn't left the school.

By now the junior high school ghost is so taken for granted that the caretaker and the principal tease each other about its existence. "When something goes wrong we say 'it's George' and sometimes [the principal] tells me [that] I'm George," she elaborated. And so George seems to be an unofficial but commonly accepted member of the junior high population.

I spoke with the mother of one of the students who has actually seen George. "My daughter said he was wearing a leather jacket when she saw him," the woman commented. She went on to explain that as George loves to play jokes on people around the school, she thinks he may be a former junior high student. "The town's first junior high school was built on that [same] spot," she said.

The building that replaced it has since been renovated and added on to, but George's presence is felt or heard or seen only in the older section of the enlarged school. This restriction isn't surprising as phantoms are usually only perceived in the area that existed when they were still flesh and blood.

In order to try to confirm her suspicions, the woman has spent quite some time poring over old school yearbooks. She did find pictures of several former students named George, but as no one seems to know why the ghost has become known by that name, her search wasn't really that enlightening. However, anonymity doesn't seem to trouble George—he continues whistling and walking and rattling his keys happily into eternity.

GHOSTLY GREETING

The man who had the bewildering experience described in this story initially indicated he would be willing to talk to me about it in greater detail. By the time I called him, however, he'd apparently changed his mind. While his change of attitude was undeniably disappointing to me, it was also understandable, considering the bizarre nature of the tale.

In northwestern Alberta, a maintenance worker was going about his rounds through the hallways of a school. He noticed a priest walking toward him. As the two passed each other, they exchanged greetings. In the course of his duties, the worker made his way to the school office. After dealing with other matters, he inquired about who the priest was with whom he had spoken earlier. The secretary had no idea who the man was referring to—there had been no visitors to the school that day.

The puzzled worker went on to discuss other matters at hand, when a photograph on the wall caught his eye. It was a picture of the priest he'd spoken to in the school hall. Hoping to prove his point that there had been a visitor to the school that day, he pointed out the man in the photograph to the office staff.

He was informed that he couldn't possibly have seen that particular priest. The worker began to argue that he was sure of what he had seen, but he was interrupted and informed that the priest in the picture had been dead for many years.

STEVIE STAYS AT HILLHURST SCHOOL

School custodians often keep log books in which they record the day's events. These journals usually contain references to matters such as weather conditions, which mechanical systems were operating during the day and under what conditions, any problems encountered with any of the school's electrical system and similar sorts of issues.

Hillhurst School in Calgary is somewhat different—it is only the second school in the province that I've come across where employees also note the activities of their resident ghost.

Considering my initial lead to this well-documented Alberta ghost story, I wasn't too surprised by its widespread acceptance. My introduction to the tale occurred while I spent a busy Saturday afternoon signing books in front of a large bookstore in West Edmonton Mall. The city was hosting a world-class figure-skating event that weekend and so the mall was crowded with tourists from all over, and many people stopped by to chat. One of those was a lady who didn't leave her name but did leave her work phone number and the enticing message that the school where she works is haunted by a very special ghost.

My initial phone call of inquiry was greeted not only with confirmation of the ghost's existence, but also with the further information that "we have his picture hanging above the door."

The school's administrative assistant then went on to tell me the ghost is the spirit of Ernest Stevenson, a former caretaker at the school. "Everyone called him Stevie. He was a great friend to the children," the woman explained. "He lived on the third floor of the school."

From the stories around Hillhurst, it sounds as though at least a part of Stevie is still in residence there.

I spoke with custodian Doug Wolfe at the school. He explained that although he has never had a direct experience with the ghost he has certainly talked to others who have.

"We have swinging doors at the tops of the stairwells," he began. "Sometimes when no one's near the doors, they'll just start to move as though someone's gone through them. One time a man came to work [at the school] first thing in the morning and he brought his son. He had the boy wait inside the school while he attended to something outside. I can't remember what it was, maybe he had to shovel a bit of snow. When he came back in, the little boy was as white as a ghost. The child said he'd seen a man."

The child's father knew that there couldn't be anyone else in the school, but he had worked there for some time and he knew the stories about Stevie continuing to roam these hallowed halls of learning. He wasn't surprised, therefore, to see the set of swinging doors nearest to where his son was standing moving back and forth, apparently of their own accord.

"He said that they were really swinging, not just moving a little bit but swinging as though someone had just gone through them," Doug commented. "I believe this occurred during a period of time when they'd taken the ghost's picture down from the school hallway. I understand a lot of things happened then."

The everyday acceptance of the beloved Stevie as a continuing presence at Hillhurst School is evident by a notation that Doug remembers reading in the log book. The fellow worker merely stated, "Saw ghost this morning."

At a time when some schools on this continent are looking to increase security, how reassuring it is to know that here in sunny Alberta at least one of our schools has its very own hall patrol.